LEARNING AND TEACHING TOGETHER

For Ann,
Jonathan and Lucy

Learning and Teaching Together

by
John M. Sutcliffe

CHESTER HOUSE PUBLICATIONS
2 Chester House, Pages Lane, London N10 1PR

First published May 1980
© John M. Sutcliffe, May 1980
ISBN 0 7150 0078 0

Printed in Great Britain by
Biddles Ltd, Guildford, Surrey

Contents

FOREWORD

This book is for everybody who is interested in Christian education. Nobody will read it without having new ideas on the subject. John Sutcliffe is well qualified for the role he has played. He is a minister of the United Reformed Church, at one time Secretary for Christian Education in the Training and Mission Department of the Congregational Church, and currently General Secretary of the Christian Education Movement. He brings both theological depth and educational insight to one of the church's most urgent questions: 'What is Christian Education?'

Perhaps few people will like all the answers because the question leads to other questions which will touch the raw nerve of cherished assumptions. Congregations may not appreciate being asked how their life style and programmes reflect the nature of God but we forget at our peril that what we do and are is a much clearer assertion (or denial) of the Gospel than what we say.

Likewise, how many churches ask themselves: 'What is the aim of Christian Education?' or, at a more homespun level, 'What are we trying to do for (or with) the children?' Readers will find some searching comments about classifying and clarifying aims, and some popular assumptions are very closely scrutinized. Nor does the author avoid the contentious issue of the place of the Bible in Christian Education. He is not satisfied with either easy answers or vague generalities, though not everybody will appreciate his boldness and clarity.

You will find here dogmatic comments that thrill, bewilder, or annoy but will certainly stimulate. The author holds his convictions strongly and argues forcibly but he also has an open mind.

This is because John Sutcliffe sees theology as a way of interpreting life. He sees the church as a community dedicated to exploring the world in the spirit of Jesus of Nazareth. The church is people and its message is about the new humanity that Christ began and which is implicit in the Kingdom of God.

What then does that say about Christian Education?

That is not a theoretical question. There are churches in Britain coming to grips with it and they are instanced in this book. This is a significant contribution to a growing and urgent debate in the Church today. Those who read it will be better able to join that debate. They will also be able to help the Church rediscover how to embody the Kingdom of God and proclaim a faith which is rich and relevant enough to attract and satisfy the enquiring minds of those who will carry that faith into the twenty-first century.

Wilfred Tooley
Secretary: Methodist Church Division of Education and Youth

May 1980

Chapter 1

Past, Present and Future

The attempts of the Church, during this century, to teach the Christian faith have been marked by contrasts. Continual development and reassessment have accompanied an almost continual decline in the number of children in the churches. There has been excitement about new educational insights and confusion about their application. A willingness to leave the Christian nurture of children to day schools and Sunday schools has begun to give way in the churches to a recognition of the church's responsibility. Once it was emphasized that children were learners and adults were teachers, now such distinctions are often denied . . .

Hamilton Archibald
Many developments in this field can be credited to individual pioneers and the first decisive new Movement in this century is associated with the name of Hamilton Archibald. His work gave new direction to Sunday schools through his insistence on teacher training, on learning from child psychology and on dividing the Sunday school into age groups. To help to develop commitment in fifteen and sixteen year olds he encouraged them to go on learning by attending a training class and assisting in work with younger children. As well as leading to a new seriousness about teaching in Sunday schools, his influence prompted them away from being predominantly a service to working-class and poorer children. As teacher training and the use of educational and psychological insights came to be accepted, so middle-class parents began to send their children to Sunday school. This move more or less coincided with the decline of family prayer, Bible reading and formal Christian teaching in middle-class homes. Many of the early students of Westhill College of Education, and indeed the College itself, the foundation of

which he inspired, remain as a testimony to Archibald's work, to the enthusiasms and pioneering spirit he engendered.

H. A. Hamilton

The second major development began with the publication in 1941 of *The Family Church in principle and practice* in which H. A. Hamilton stressed the importance of relating the Sunday school to the life of the church. He laid emphasis on relationships in teaching, on giving children an opportunity to share in the worship of the church and on kindling their imagination about the nature and purpose of the fellowship of faith. According to Hamilton, who found inspiration in the Orthodox Churches, what a child experiences of the total church community is more important than what he is taught. The carefully prepared learning and teaching programme is only a part of something larger. This total experience gathers meaning from many different elements. Among these may be an experience of true worship, a sense of being wanted and cared for, an appreciation of beauty and a dawning recognition that this company of people have certain priorities in the way they use their time and money. There may be a rich knowledge of and fellowship with other people through the sharing of views and common interests, a bearing of disagreements in love and a sense of being involved in a community which has mighty purposes in the locality and throughout the world. Conversely, children will sometimes have a sense of church premises being vast and dull and neglected, of overhearing gossip, of being bored by trivia or defeated by the apparent irrelevance of experience in church to daily life.

Some of H. A. Hamilton's major concerns were expressed in *The Religious needs of children in care* and again in 1961 in *Communication and the Christian Community.* 'The Gospel of the incarnation needs a community or it has no living language. This community must be exposed to the world of contemporary need and opportunity or it cannot speak so as to be heard . . . We do not communicate by explaining; only by translating . . . there can be no community where men are not open to each other; willing to be known to each other; to receive from each other as well as to give; ready to be involved, for Christ's sake, in each other's need; to stand behind each other at the place of every man's encounter with the world . . . Young people growing up in such a community would be in no doubt that the Gospel was not "a good idea of God's" but a transforming energy."[1]

Hamilton's influence is to be seen not only where, predominantly in Free Churches, people strive to apply his principles of Family Church, but also at Westhill College where he was Principal. To the College, during his time, there came a cluster of men and women the influence of whose work has been far-reaching.

Ronald Goldman

Dr. Ronald Goldman's research into *Religious Thinking from Childhood to Adolescence* was published in 1964 and followed in 1965 by *Readiness for Religion*. Goldman described how far children of varying ages, abilities and backgrounds can understand religious concepts. The research was undertaken in day schools using Bible stories and concepts of the Church, prayer and God which were common to many Agreed Syllabuses in use at the time. It showed how easily children could misunderstand what was being taught when the ideas used were in advance of their stage of development. Goldman's work was influential in causing a total review of the content of teaching generally, and especially of the content suitable for young children.

His colleague, Dr. Kenneth Hyde, modified Goldman's findings, suggesting they may be valid for children in school, but not necessarily valid for children coming from a Christian home. Such children, he argued, have an experience which gives them greater insight into the meaning of religious concepts.

The experiential approach

Stimulated by the work of H. A. Hamilton and Ronald Goldman, Douglas Hubery wrote a booklet, *The Experiential Approach to Christian Education*, and contributed to two accounts of experiments undertaken by Westhill staff, *Experience and Worship* (8–11 year olds) and *Living and Praising* (11–14 year olds). In a further book, *Teaching the*

Christian Faith Today, published in 1965, Hubery wrote, 'The vast majority of people learn through the whole of their personalities, their senses, their relationships. The greater the sense of participation and involvement in a situation, the more one's faculties are exercised in that situation, the deeper becomes embedded into life the lessons being taught in that situation. There are certain high moments, for good or ill, when we say, "I'll never forget this as long as I live" . . . we have indeed learned from experience . . . experience is a happening in life which in varying degrees affects the whole of our being, body, mind and soul. It is a dimension of learning which we can never afford to ignore or bypass. The experiential approach to education seeks to ensure that what is taught is not mere subjective emotion, nor objective intellectualism; it is both and more than both. It is teaching which affects the whole of one's being'(page 58).[2] Hubery's work brought together the strands of research in an educational approach of remarkable wholeness. It sought to give real significance to what was taught recognizing that children need to explore their experience and to be helped to encounter the deepest and highest dimensions of meaning.

The *Partners in Learning* and *Alive in God's World* courses, based on the experiential approach, were published in 1968 and began the third major development in the teaching of the faith in churches in this century. It should be noted in passing that the work undertaken at Westhill College was related both to Religious Education in the day schools and to Christian education in the churches. No major research has been undertaken since then into Christian education as such. In the meantime a marked distinction has developed between Religious and Christian education. Thus, today, when the State sponsors and funds research into school Religious Education, that research is less likely to be applicable to the churches' task. There is now an urgent need for resources to finance research into Christian education.

The sixties were a period of theological and social, as well as educational, upheaval. The publication of John Robinson's *Honest to God* in 1963 or Nathaniel Micklem's *Religion for Agnostics* can serve to symbolize the former. A feature of the theology of the sixties was not simply that it asked questions in new ways, open to the contemporary intellectual challenges to belief, but that it showed a determination to take the secular world seriously. This shift in the method and content of theology reflected both a fresh honesty about ways to interpret and express the Gospel, and an underlying failure of confidence. This was, and is, important for Christian education; it is no longer confined to the traditional tasks of communicating the faith of the fathers to a new generation. It is now theologically respectable for teachers to urge pupils to explore and interpret their own experience in the light of the Gospel and thereby create theology for themselves.

The social upheaval, marked by prosperity in the West, increasing mobility, a critical attitude in institutions, a questioning of authority, a growing influence of Eastern religions and oriental styles of meditation in traditionally Christian countries, and the development of a powerful youth culture, also helped to rock the church's confidence. Between 1968 and 1973 the decline of the churches was by as much as one third of the children attending church and one fifth of the confirmed membership.

'The Story of the People of God'

By the early seventies there was a new willingness to tackle theological questions and a deep concern about the number and the place of children in the church. Evidence of this was to be found in two working party reports published in 1976. Both reports refer back to the work of H. A. Hamilton and stress the importance of the child's experience in the church community. *The Story of the People of God*[3] argues the continuity and corporateness of the Christian tradition and communicates a much needed sense of certitude, while supporting experimental and experiential attitudes to education. The sense of security, on which adventure may be based, is important. Its message is a corrective to the individualism inherited from the last century. But *The Story of the People of God* fails in its grappling with the central issue of how the Bible may be used systematically in both teaching and worship.

Since the publication of Goldman's research there has remained an uncertainty about the use of the Bible. Leaders are uncertain about the age at which children are ready to experience different kinds of literature. It is generally accepted, for instance, that children under twelve years of age cannot handle parables and that the use of language should follow upon and describe experience rather than precede it. In practice, both these views raise considerable dilemmas for leaders. Where the guide lines are not clear there are many more problems. For example, should children be told Bible stories because these stories are part of the Christian heritage even though the stories may not be understood? Leaders of children's groups are divided as to whether a story like that of Noah, which young children enjoy but cannot understand, should be told so that it becomes part of their cultural memory.

Scholars are used to treating the Bible as an ordinary book. Like many others, it is a book to explore, to study and to enjoy. Students and people of faith need to have a sense of the broad sweep of the story as well as to study it in detail. Difficulties arise when the Bible is treated as a 'different' kind of book. The compilers of lectionaries break it up into short passages intended for daily or weekly reading and enjoin congregations 'to sit under the word'. The implication is that we suspend all our usual faculties of appreciation, enjoyment, criticism and historical judgment and try to hear it as a direct message from God for our time. Thus the Bible is not reacted to in the way that we react to other books. These different approaches are important and should be examined. Research is still needed into more creative ways of linking the use of the Bible in teaching and liturgy and into the significance of the telling of the Bible as a story.

Perhaps above all, a new style of lectionary is needed. The possibility of a lectionary based on, say, a four rather than a two year cycle might be explored. Between the major Christian festivals the lectionary would be thematic. As well as providing lections for the festivals and themes for use in the church's liturgy, a fairly large number of other relevant Bible passages would be listed together with passages suitable for use with particular age groups and for use in family worship. Such a lectionary could be used in both the church's liturgy and education programme; much more of the Bible would be read and used than is common with existing lectionaries.

'The Child in the Church'

The second report mentioned above came from The Child in the Church Working Party. The Working Party was asked to note current thinking in the Churches about the Christian education of children in the context of the local church and community and to assess means whereby children are nurtured in the Christian faith. The report takes seriously the complexity of contemporary society in which the making of responsible Christian decisions is never a straightforward exercise. The Working Party was acutely aware of the way in which people learn – more by doing than by hearing or seeing. *The Child in the Church*[4] reflects a growing awareness that the churches must take more seriously their responsibility to teach the faith. Clear distinctions are made between the purpose of Religious Education in school and of Christian education in the family and church. The report has gone into several editions and been the basis of much discussion at congregational as well as synodical levels.

The Child in the Church argues strongly that children are part of the church. 'Children are a gift to the Church. The Lord of the Church sets them in the midst of the church, today as in Galilee, not as objects of benevolence, nor even as recipients of instruction, but in the last analysis as patterns of discipleship. The church that does not accept children unconditionally into the fellowship is depriving those children of what is rightfully theirs, but the deprivation such a church will itself suffer is far more grave.' The emphasis throughout is on the nurture of children, indeed it is argued that what happens in church cannot properly be called education. 'Christian nurture is one of the terms used to describe every-thing which aids this process of growth. It may include study of the Bible (2 Timothy 3.14–17), the ministry of preachers and teachers (1 Corinthians 14.26) . . . We understand Christian nurture first of all when we see that it springs out of the nature of the Christian life itself as a process of contin-uous growth. This growth does not take place in isolation, but in company with others who are also walking in the same way. Our understanding of nurture is thus bound up with our

understanding of the church, the community of the way . . .
Secular education and Christian nurture have this in common:
they both seek to give the child his past so as to enable him to
create his own future. But whereas education conceives of
this future broadly in terms of the values of our liberal
democracy, Christian nurture conceives of it in terms of the
Christian future . . . Christian nurture occupies a middle
position between closed and authoritative instruction on the
one hand, in which the past is simply reduplicated, and open,
enquiring education on the other.'

Nurture and Education

I understand by the word 'nurture', the support of the
individual by the loving, caring relationships of the community of the church and the communication, through a
person's participation in the church's life, its aims, its
visions and its priorities. Nurture is closely linked with what
is implicit in the community's life, with conversation and the
sympathetic process of involvement. A child who is the only
church attender in a day school class of thirty children needs
the nurture of carefully thought out support. Children having,
almost inevitably, a strong sense of the immediacy and
importance of the present moment and its news and problems,
need the nurture of a community with a mature historic
perspective. Nurture as support or incorporation into a tradition is easy to understand. I am less satisfied with this
emphasis on nurture when what is meant is teaching. At this
point the report's own rigid definitions of nurture and education seem to cause difficulties. Neither is satisfactory. Why
restrict education to mean only formal learning of a
particularly enquiring, critical sort? To my mind education
implies a process of sharing and discovery which at times will
appeal to and involve all aspects of the person – the critical
faculty, emotions, aesthetic sense, ability to weigh evidence
and to make decisions.

Moreover, is not the educative task of the church far wider
than nurture as defined by *The Child in the Church*? Nurture
may give children a working knowledge of the faith, ways of
doing things and looking at things which spring from the
Christian tradition. But it hardly describes the rigorous

process of assimilating information on which mature judgments can be made – and the church cannot do without this sort of rigour. Often the nature of the subject under consideration, say, Paul's teaching about women, requires an open, critical approach.

In other words, nurture may aptly describe a kind of sympathetic upbringing within the family of faith, but is not adequate to describe all that young people need in their growth to maturity. For example, a leader working with adolescents must allow for and encourage free-wheeling exploration which does not presuppose commitment. Family Church in practice was good at nurturing young people. One criticism of it was that it failed, as have other systems, in intellectual rigour. Some young people who had been used to the loving support of the church in their home locality were singularly unable to cope with the critical stress of, for instance, university life.

Part of the problem arises because nurture is normally assumed to aim at fostering commitment. But the leader who encourages an exploring, enquiring approach has to reckon with the possibility that the young people may reject the church permanently because of it. To that extent what he does is as open-ended as any other educational process. Further, the church will sometimes be engaged in teaching which, as regards commitment, is neutral. For instance, anyone who seeks to understand the controversy about the ordination of women will probably study Jewish customs in Biblical times, the attitude of the Early Fathers to women and that of the medieval church. Study of this kind has little to do with being nurtured into Christian faith!

Church and School

Having suggested some drawbacks of using education and nurture in limited senses, I propose to use the term 'Christian education', but to limit its meaning to the church's part in teaching, and teaching about, the Christian faith. I am not concerned here with what might constitute a complete education in accordance with Christian principles and insights. It may help us to mark the distinction between Religious Education in schools and Christian education as practised in church. The respective roles of these two aspects of education can be described as follows:

In Religious Education the pupil is involved in an exploration of religions. Religion is included in the curriculum because like number, language, music, art or the physical world, it is part of human experience. The pupil may celebrate with his classmates, aspects of many religious festivals. If he has no connection with or knowledge of a religious institution all these will be strange to him, except perhaps in the most popular sense Christmas. If he has a religious affiliation, the practices of other faiths or religious groups will be strange to him. Questions will be probed and the pupil will be involved in discovering how different communities of faithful people communicate their faith, learn their faith, and worship. Such an exploration will eventually enable him to understand something of the connection between religion and culture, and religion in contemporary issues. Religious Education may develop also a respect for people who have different beliefs and different ways of doing things from those he has grown to hold. The open exploration of ideas and practices may have sparked the pupil to admiration or to faith, to find his own life style or to accept a particular philosophy of life, though such commitment will not have been the aim of the teacher nor may the teacher know what has happened. While the nature of commitment in the major world faiths should be studied, the commitment of the pupil is a private matter as far as the teaching of Religious Education is concerned.

In the United Kingdom, with its long Christian tradition, most time will be spent in studying Christianity. The pupil will become familiar with parts of the Bible, he will study the church locally and more widely, hear some of the stories of people of faith and see some of the links between Christian faith and British institutions and English literature. He will discover that some of his questions about life and meaning are those to which Christianity offers clues. And in all this, he will exercise his critical faculties, appreciating that which is to be appreciated but accepting nothing simply because it exists or on another's authority.

In short, Religious Education should enable a pupil to

understand that religion is thought by very many people, but not all, to be a part of the 'given' in human life: it is important enough in human experience to be taken seriously. The pupil will learn about religions or a particular religious faith; but school will not give him an experience of faith.

In the church, the child will explore the background and meaning of the community through learning and learning about, the Bible, the history of the Church and its spread and work, and the lives of notable Christians. He will be encouraged to feel himself a part of the historic community and of the future mission. He will be helped to discover what it means to practice the faith, though he himself may not have faith, through service of others, prayer, worship and the practice of generosity. He may well be critical of much that he experiences and is taught, but none-the-less he will be caught up in the celebration of Christ present in his church (where two or three are gathered together) as well as in the historic (Jesus of Nazareth).

The task of the church, which is life long, is to communicate such a vision of life, faith, and the world as will fascinate the child (or person of any age) enough to win his allegiance or incite enough curiosity as to suggest it might be worthwhile sticking with it. That is, the child will both learn about the faith and participate in it; an aim of the church will be to give the child an experience of faith.

Continuity and Community

Each of the developments I have described has given new impetus to the teaching of the faith and each has built on the strengths of what has gone before. For all the emphasis put from time to time on new approaches, there has been a strong sense of continuity. This must be emphasized as we now turn our attention to the future. Ever since the early forties attention has been given to the community of the church. It was there in the 1974 Report of a WCC Conference, *Learning Community*. It is there in the recent Reports. Since 1975 the *Partners in Learning* courses have been subtitled 'A Church community education programme'. The weight of evidence suggests that the next step in Christian education must take us into a new experience of the church being a

worshipping, learning, teaching, serving and witnessing
community in which people of all ages are engaged together.
It will mean taking seriously insights into the use of experience, the appropriateness of content, the importance of
security and tradition as well as of freedom to adventure and
explore, and the place of children in the church. If we accept
that adults as well as children are learners in the faith, we
must go on to discover what it means to say that the church
is a 'learning community'. The liturgical and educational
consequences for adults of receiving children as one of God's
gifts to the church must be faced. It must be remembered
that the verb 'to learn' is always active and personal to the
speaker. It is not only good grammar that prevents us from
saying 'I learned him'; in the last analysis no one can make
learning happen except the learner himself! The test of local
church life will be its quality not its size – a church of two
hundred and fifty people may be big enough if there is to be
real corporate life. But how can a local church help people to
have such a variety of experience as will enable them to
appreciate the rich diversity of catholic and protestant,
radical and conservative traditions? How can teachers and
other adults be helped to discover that they must learn from
children, and to accept the liberation and vitality children
bring to corporate life?

The next step
    The developments we have described contain the seeds
not only of the next steps in nurture and teaching but a next
step in the whole life of the church as well. We shall discuss
aspects of this in the next chapters. But what terms shall we
use to describe what we are talking about? The connotations
of 'Sunday school' prevent its use now that we are thinking
of children as part of the church. In any case we are pointing
to something more than 'school'. 'Family Church' is misleading, not least because it caused some people to think it
meant the church was a family of families, rather than to see
'family' as referring to the importance of relationships within
the Christian community. Moreover, we are concerned with
something more than loving and sensitive relationships.
Terms like 'lay training' and 'laity formation' communicate

neither educational nor theological sense. 'Church community education programme' is pretentious and gives no clue that it must be as much about worship as about education, about individuals as about the community. 'In-church education', a term I favoured in *Learning Community*, is similarly prejudiced. Fundamentally we are concerned with the complex matter of how the church explores, shares, celebrates and lives its faith, and in particular how this refers to learning and teaching. We are concerned with the nature of the church!

Chapter 2

Being the Church

To Jews at the time of Jesus children were important not as themselves but as the future people of Israel. *The Child in the Church* report argues that Jesus challenged this view by teaching that the Kingdom belongs to children and adults: those who in a trusting dependence can say, 'Abba'. The childhood of Jesus confers infinite worth on childhood; it argues, 'whether at ten years, ten months or ten days, there is a right relationship to God fitted to that age. . . . A child at any age may be wholly human and wholly God's. Because Christ was a child, a child can be a Christian'.

This view differs sharply from those often expressed in churches. Perhaps the quickest way of discovering a church's attitude to children is to ask about the place of children in the celebration of Holy Communion. Children are said to be not ready to participate in Holy Communion because they do not understand, or are not yet committed to Christ, or cannot accept the responsibilities of adult membership of the church. Arbitrary decisions have been made about the appropriate age for Confirmation: about seven years, early teens, late teens.

We appear not to have moved all that far away from the view of children common in the time of Charles Dickens. The lives of Dickens' many child characters – Oliver Twist, Little Nell, Paul Dombey, David Copperfield – are determined by adults who think of them as unprofitable economic units. This view was implicitly rooted in the Calvinism and the Benthamism of the eighteenth century. It meant in practice that children were treated as though they were sinful creatures who by memorizing knowledge and learning the wisdom of their elders would grow into useful members of society. Some might even become Christian! Dickens' world of love and imagination challenged this view, so for instance in the first part of *Dombey and Son* there is a

New Testament parable of love being found among the weak and simple.

Implications of our belief in God

What we believe about God determines the way we think of the church. What a church believes about itself and its people ultimately depends on its view of God. In the last resort our belief in God is, by definition, an act of faith. We may speak about it in as rational a manner as possible. We may try to show that believing in God is not unreasonable or is no more unreasonable than adopting any other view of life. But on whatever evidence we may base our believing, the actual attitude of belief is one of profound trust. The evidence for faith, for Christians, is likely to come from the Bible, the story of the world church, experience in the church, fellowship with people of faith and more general reflection on life experience. Such diversity of experience leads none-the-less to a remarkable unity in the way Christian people express their faith. Many particular experiences and convictions which individually may be relatively insignificant – but through which, some would say, God addresses us – enable us to formulate a view of the nature of God. We then have to discover the implications of this view for the particular circumstances of daily life.

Through the life and teaching of Jesus we know God as a Father who in love gave and gives himself to his children. He does not force himself or his will on to them, nor does he claim to be omni-competent. He offers himself and his gift of the future as an opportunity they may accept or reject. Through Jesus we learn to think of God both as a person and a way. Jesus' attitude is life-affirming. He sets people free to choose. God is a Father who because of his loving care suffers for and with his people. He is known as the fellowship of the Trinity. His unwillingness to force himself on his children and the making of the old and new covenants show his respect for his children, whom he treats as though they are able to act responsibly.

If that is how we understand the nature of God we would expect the life of his Church to reflect it; to be marked by love, care, self-giving, openness to people and to life, a deep sense of fellowship, a willingness to suffer, and a notable sense of responsibility. There is nothing in our understanding of the nature of God to suggest that God is more interested in people of a certain age or with particular abilities, than in others. His nature concentrates our attention on the meaning of persons and communities, not on childhood or age. His way concentrates our attention on the realities of ordinary life and the decisions we make that affect our future.

Presuppositions about the church

In all that follows we shall be making a number of pre-suppositions about the life of the church in a locality. For instance, that the church is held together and motivated by a living faith and that when its members speak of teaching the faith they are intending us to think of the exploration of a process rather than a body of knowledge only. We shall need to know something about the living tradition of the past, but this must be balanced by the actual experience of the church, the community of faith. So, questions are raised such as – What is its faith? And what does it mean to be involved in this Christian process of being and becoming, this perspective for hearing, looking and acting? What difference does it all make to the future which is both a gift and is yet waiting to be created? In *A Rumour of Angels* Peter L. Berger drew attention to the importance of the community of faith:[5] 'It follows that the community (or, more exactly, communities) in which Christ becomes manifest cannot be identified with any particular "names" or traditions though He may be more manifest in some than in others. The presence of Christ will have to be determined not by a direct succession from a certain point of the past, but rather from such evidence as can be found in the empirical reality of communities whose actions can be called redemptive. Wherever communities gather around acts of redeeming love, there we may look for the presence of Christ. The redemptive community of Christ in the world must be seen as ever coming into being again in the empirical history of man. It will be there implicitly wherever these gestures are understood in relation to the God who both created and redeems the world, who may well have been "in Jesus", but who is ever again present in the human imitations of redemptive love. Every such community, whether implicitly in its actions or explicitly in its worship, anticipates here and now the consummation of redemption towards which the world is moving.'

All learners

We shall presuppose also that everyone in the church, not children only, are learners. It is of the nature of children that they are learners, but all must learn to say, 'Abba'. Christian commitment involves us in a process of growth which is an adventure of faith. In the personal process of finding and maintaining faith and of thinking in a Christian way about living, we are helped by the experience, wisdom, insight, questions, criticism and faithfulness of the whole community. In this learning community we shall think of the children as being part of the church today, not the church of tomorrow only. In some communions it is possible to emphasize that in Baptism a child becomes a member of the church. Confirmation or adult church membership enables him to make clear his own chosen position and to share in the government of the church. But confirmation and church membership are not points of arrival only, they are launching-pads for further growth and adventure in faith. The mission of God in the world is an activity whose tomorrow cannot be described today. Conscious participation in it through confirmation or church membership always involves us in corporate as well as individual action. Through its commitment to people, to prayer, to wrestling with meanings and implications and its trying to respond sensitively to contemporary life, the church helps to shape the future – the creation of which is part of the mission of God. To be involved in such an activity, at whatever age, is to be involved also in a process of growth or learning which is both experiential and active.

All teachers

It is not easy for many adults to accept the idea that in a community composed of children and adults all are teachers, as well as learners. It has been common practice to appoint adults to teach the children, but not the reverse. Sometimes the contribution of adolescents to the church is recognised:

they lead worship, make music, provoke adults to deeper thought with their questions and opinions. They demand action of the church in matters of social concern, and evangelism. Those who are confirmed or become church members may be allowed into the councils of the church. But it has not been supposed that they have much to teach the church. This is sad; for instance, many of the early 1970s generation of young people were united in social action and in the singing of folk songs which expressed concern and hope about the world. This spontaneous young people's movement was largely ignored by the church, which is all the more a pity since, as the decade ended, young people were being criticized for their complacency and conformism.

Jesus tells us that children show us the way into the kingdom of heaven. For Jesus, children were his hearers' teachers. They have a practical part to play in teaching adults in the church community. Sometimes they liberate adults, enabling them to take part in an activity in which they are not practised. Sometimes their observations and questions illuminate a point vividly. Their willingness to learn, to trust, to talk openly and without affectation about the deeper things in life, to worship simply and completely, their sense of fun and hope, all have much to teach adults. But only if children are accepted fully as persons.

If children can help adults to see things in a new light, the process can happen in reverse especially when children and adults are working together. In such a mixed age group, children seem able to grasp the meaning of ideas and concerns which could not be introduced to a peer group.

Christians need each other

I take it for granted that the church is needed! Whatever theological arguments may be brought to justify its existence, the church exists because experience demands that it should exist. Christians need each other. We are unable, for instance, to discover the hidden riches of the Bible, to relate faith to life, to construct Christian views and judgments, to engage in large scale social action, or to celebrate the sacraments on our own. For many people experience in the church community is the decisive experience. By what the church is and does, the life of faith, Christian values and priorities are demonstrated and shared. Limited and partial though the life of a local church may be, it points to a meaning and to a way beyond itself. For instance, the church may offer to the world an example of a society in which persons are accepted for their own sake, not because of goodness, ability or attainments. To the extent that it does that, it points to its own faith in an accepting God.

The language and imagery of the school are not adequate to describe experience in the church. By what it is, the community of faith will at its best share a vision of life and a sense of purpose in life. It will communicate a sense of continuity throughout history. It will be involved in its neighbourhood yet also help people to have a sense of the world dimension of the love and work of God. It will demonstrate the importance of persons and the gentler emotions. By what it is in the experience of those who are part of it or are influenced by it, the church communicates and teaches – for good or ill – more than by what it says.

If it is to express the life-affirming attitude of Jesus, the church will need to maintain flexibility in its organization, use of resources and times of meeting. And, if it is to be true to experience, the church will have to cultivate a new openness. No longer can its predominating style be that of proclamation. This must be balanced by humble listening, sharing, and seeking.

A 1965 report re-assessing H. A. Hamilton's description of the church as a family is still worthy of consideration.[6] The local church is described as:

(*a*) The organ of new Christian life, the community within which we expect the children of God to be born again and to be trained in the truth of God in Christ.

(*b*) The organ of mission, since it is of the nature of the family to grow. This for the church usually means a going out, persistently, in service to others, offering to them all that God has given in Christ, which includes membership in the family of the church.

(*c*) The agency for the care of God's people, nurturing those young in age towards faith, feeding and training those young in discipleship. But such caring cannot be limited to those within the family, for Christ is also the head of all humanity, and his people are called to care for all.

(*d*) A fellowship in which young and old interact to their mutual benefit.

(*e*) A stable society in which young and old find security, strength, reassurance and encouragement, and at the same time an outgoing society, sending its members out to serve and challenging them to service.

(*f*) A redeeming fellowship, exerting a healing influence in its outgoing; but also something to which its members come for renewal and recreation, and in which others from outside can find the same healing and restoring power.

(*g*) A relationship of persons who experience occasions when suffering of one or more is accepted as necessary for the good of all, and in which all suffering can be borne in a better spirit because of mutual care.

Taking people seriously

The church must communicate its intention to take people seriously for their own sake. Whether or not the churches have ever been trusted by the majority of people is a matter for discussion; but the establishing of trust depends on there being integrity between the church's words and actions. It takes little insight, for instance, to perceive that a ghetto life is not likely to communicate the life of love which is seen in Jesus. The churches have been ready to welcome those who fit with social ease into their fellowships, but people who might not fit in have sometimes been seriously neglected.

Flexibility in church life will be required for it to be free enough to take people seriously and offer them a real opportunity to learn by participating. Every time a church responds sensitively to people, its own life is risked and changed. The quality of experience a person is able to find within this creative community of trust and faith is of paramount importance to his understanding of Christianity. This suggests there should be a balance in the church's programme, which will probably involve a move away from the domination of church life by formal worship. If the church meets only for worship and if that worship is conceived in formal terms, the church communicates only a very partial view of the gospel. A nine year old was asked why he had stopped going to church after three years of regular church attending. He shrugged his shoulders and dismissed the experience easily, saying, 'Well, it's all hymns and prayers, isn't it?' It seems unlikely that a nine year old who had spent some hundred and fifty hours with Jesus could have left with that impression. We cannot simplistically justify what we do now in church life by direct reference to the New Testament, but the diversity of church life described in the Acts of the Apostles is bound to be of interest.

Participation: children and adults

In a report (1971) on the use of the British Lessons Council's syllabus, *Experience and Faith*, Philip Cliff said, 'Perhaps the most urgent question to be now engaged in is how we can get a closer involvement of parents, children and young people, so that the educational value of being in a live community will be seen, felt and so deeply experienced that children as they grow to their time of forming values, will want of themselves to belong to the family of Christ in which they have been nurtured.' In that quotation I would prefer the word 'adults' in place of 'parents'. In practice the involvement of which Philip Cliff speaks could mean that a local church will no longer take it for granted that all the children's groups will meet on Sunday, or that adults and children will remain separated. Before asking how it will teach the children and what this will mean for a particular age group, the church will first ask: How can we all tackle this theme, be involved in this celebration, or be engaged by and listen to this part of the Bible together?

This will demand of leaders imaginative and sensitive thought about experiences that children and adults have in common, or could have in common, through shared activity. They will ask, in what ways can adults and children free each other, enjoy corporate activity, or in the broadest sense teach each other? They will ask, Are there conversations children ought to have the opportunity to overhear? Such questions as these should be answered before leaders go on to discuss at what points the church needs to divide into age groups. In this the leaders will be guided by such things as the children's limitations of language and experience or their special need of peer groups. The traditional liturgy may be used in its full or shortened form, but the leaders will have to discuss how activity and conversation might lead into, or grow out of, worship.

The answers given to these questions may mean that one church will continue with a pattern which looks remarkably traditional whereas another church will develop new patterns of community life and activity. Many churches are now experimenting with new forms of worship and new programmes of learning and serving, despite the church's tendency to close ranks in periods of decline. It is important that this is the case. Churches should be able to respond, especially in times of rapid social change, to local circumstances and to create a community life that is appropriate in those circumstances.

And what about a sense of tradition in those churches which are looking for new ways of expressing Christian community and discipleship? A new style of life itself should be an authentic expression of the living Christian tradition. Churches which meet in old buildings, ancient parish churches or classical expressions of reformation churchmanship, have special advantages over others. But all churches have their story to tell and that story is part of the teaching resource. The local story has a place along with the wider story, the classical formulations of faith, Christian doctrine and the tenets of a particular communion, in the communication of a sense of the tradition. However, real awareness of the Christian tradition does not depend on meeting in old premises or on the use of particular formularies and ceremonies, but on actually participating in the tradition. It would be as great an impoverishment to concentrate exclusively on the past as it would be to assume that only the present is important. Participation in a balanced local community of faith should give a person a sense of being part of the covenant people, the body of Christ, the fellowship of the Holy Spirit and the mission of God – the living tradition.

Openness

The fact that Christianity is an historic faith contributes both to the sense of security experienced by believers and to their confusion and uncertainty. The traditional formulations of the faith were written in a language appropriate to their authors' understanding of the world. Now, many disciples of Jesus feel unable simply to recite such formulations from the New Testament or the early church. The problem is partly one of language; it is difficult to interpret for our own day words like 'saviour', 'lord', 'only begotten', 'resurrection of the body'. It is also partly that of our uncertainty about how to use history. We are faced with such questions as: How can we now enter into the experience of, say, the members of the earliest churches? How can we understand their experience of faith and its relation to their experience in and understanding of the world? Do some ways of understanding their experience and of making use of it in our own time have more integrity than others?

More people have received Secondary and Higher Education in the past thirty years than ever before. Part of the function of education is to help people to ask intelligent questions and to be more open and honest with themselves. We should not be disappointed if educated men and women bring their openness and honesty into church life. In the long run it will make for a healthier and more firmly grounded faith. But in the meantime, it will require of the church a willingness to be more open to questions about the fundamentals of faith and more understanding of those who ask uncomfortable questions. To ask for flexibility in the way faith is expressed is to run the risk of being misunderstood – is nothing any longer sacred? – but it is a risk which must be taken. People should be able to think of the church as the place where important questions are welcomed. It is more important that the church communicates its willingness openly and honestly to search and investigate than that it maintains a façade of seeming to know all the answers. Moreover, a mature community will be able to show that this is the way to a deeper sense of security which can cope with uncertainties and the conflict of rival claims.

A number of examples of how churches have tried to

develop their learning and teaching ministry are included in Chapter 6.

The Church

I called this brief chapter, 'On Being the Church'. I have tried to suggest that developments in education and in theological understanding combine to direct the church into new ways of expressing its corporate worship, learning and work. I was persuaded when I was writing *Learning Community* not to head a chapter, 'The Death of the Sunday School'! Instead it became, 'The Life and Death of the Sunday School?' In my view it is now inappropriate to speak of Sunday school, because to do so and to maintain an institution which is in even a minor way separate from the church, seriously distorts the nature of the church. It also deprives children – and others in the church – of necessary experience. It tends to hold up the development of new forms of Christian community activity. Sunday school is not only inappropriate, it is an inheritance we no longer need and for our own good we should let it go. We need churches!

Now we shall turn our attention to the individuals who compose the church. Then we shall discuss the aims of the church's teaching programme and the place of the Bible in it, before looking at developments in church life and preparation for leadership.

Chapter 3

Real People

The title of this chapter was suggested by Carl Roger's important book, *On becoming a person*. He writes, 'The more I am open to the realities in me and in the other person, the less do I find myself wishing to rush in to "fix things" . . . Experience is for me the highest authority. The touchstone of validity in my own experience. No other person's ideas, and none of my own ideas, are as authoritative as my experience . . . Neither the Bible nor the prophets – neither Freud nor research – neither the revelations of God nor man – can take precedence over my own direct experience . . . My experience is not authoritative because it is infallible. It is the basis of authority because it can always be checked in new primary ways. In that way its frequent error of fallibility is always open to correction'.[7]

From the Gospel portraits of Jesus we learn that he took both the group and the individual with ultimate seriousness. Much that we say about learning and teaching in church is inevitably concerned with the group and the interplay of experience in the group. But groups are made up of individuals. Churches are made up of individuals. In this chapter I shall try to balance my inevitable emphasis on the group by considering personal development and the authority of personal experience. To do this I shall draw on the work of psychologists.

Stages of development
The work of Jean Piaget has been most influential in affecting our understanding of development. He has described human development as falling into four stages. Stage one, the first two years of life, he calls sensorimotor intelligence. During this time the child is driven by the need to fulfil his physical and emotional needs. He calls for food; he claims the attention of his parents. He may begin to understand the

meaning of sound but not of language.

Stage two, the years three to six, is described as the years of pre-logical thought, 'The stage of intuitive intelligence, of spontaneous inter-personal feelings and of social relationships in which the child is subordinate to the adult'.

Stage three, the years seven to eleven or twelve years of age, he describes as the stage of concrete conceptual operations. During these years the child begins to think logically and to argue logically. Rules are accepted as being fixed though the older children in this group are beginning to challenge the rules and rulemakers. These years are crucial for the child's understanding of the social and political process.

Stage four, the adolescent years, Piaget characterizes as years of abstract intelligence operations. Rules become principles and principles can be argued about and changed. This is the 'stage of . . . the formation of the personality, and of effective and intellectual entry into the society of adults'.[8]

Child studies

Piaget's analysis is based on years of patient research. Awareness of this or of other research does not excuse the church worker from reflecting on his own experience of people. A most fascinating study has been undertaken by the World Lutheran Federation of the age level characteristics of children, young people and young adults, in churches in the United States of America, Tamilnadu in India, Liberia, the Middle East, South Africa and Tanzania. People in ninety-one churches contributed. The study was intended to lead to the preparation of more appropriate teaching material. Physical, emotional, intellectual, social and religious characteristics were observed. The reports show remarkable similarities between people of the same age despite the very different backgrounds of those observed. A stimulating tabulation was published by the Secretariat for Christian Education in 1975.[9]

Many leaders have found it illuminating to undertake a series of child studies. Through these they have been able to gain insights into development at different stages of growth. The practice of limiting child study to the age group the leader is most used to working with is unfortunate. It is even more unfortunate that many ministers and clergy have never undertaken a child study other than that of their own children. The *Equipped to Teach*[10] course counsels would-be students, 'when you have carefully prepared for your study, you should keep a dated, weekly diary of all your observations of the child, both in the department and in any contacts you may have during the week'. It is important to keep detailed observations. Suggestions for these are as follows: 'Actual conversation between the child and yourself or other adults, and between the child and other children. Detailed accounts of situations involving co-operation or hostility between the child and yourself, or other adults, and between the child and other children. Detailed accounts of situations in which the child shows confidence, fear, anxiety, happiness, etc. Actual questions asked and comments made about stories, pictures, nature objects, music, etc. Detailed descriptions of the child's response in worship in church and department. Accounts of his response to beautiful objects or situations, for instance, flowers, music, etc. Detailed descriptions of the way the child sets about a task, for instance, how he makes a model, plays a part in dramatisation, etc.'

Whether or not we undertake such studies, the more we listen to children, young people and adults, the more we shall be able to discover about their thought processes and feelings. And until we do know something about these we are unlikely to be able to communicate well. If, for instance, a youth understands relationships and the meaning of authority mainly through his experience in a football team, that is the experience on which the leader will have to build in talking about relations or authority. Or if a man under-stands security only in terms of money and his ability to manipulate affairs, that attitude to life will have to be sensitively explored and understood before he will be able to take the next step towards personal fulfilment. Such encounters with people can be enriched by our awareness of the work of psychologists. In a healthy person each stage of development builds on the preceding stage. Stages which are, so to speak, rushed through or omitted, constitute the basis of emotional problems in adult life.

Piaget's research, like the later research into the religious development of children which was based on it, is slightly less than satisfactory for the church leader. Insufficient account was taken of experience in community. For instance, a group which included two middle-aged men, a housewife, a younger man, a nine year old girl and a six year old boy, were engaged in preparing Christmas cards which were to be sent from the church to political prisoners in Rhodesia. As they worked together they talked about the kind of greeting it was appropriate to write on the cards. They discussed the prisoners' plight and the meaning of imprisonment for them and their families. Afterwards over lunch, the six year old began a conversation about ways in which people show care and compassion. His perception had been greatly increased because he had been working with a mixed age group; his questions and concerns were of a kind that could not have been provoked by a peer group activity for six year olds. Further research is needed to help us to understand the effect on development and perception of various kinds of community experience. Experience leads me not to place 'effective and intellectual entry into the society of adults' so late in development (see stage four above[11]). Further, at least one major psychologist has described development somewhat differently, saying that in terms of intelligence measured at seventeen years of age, fifty per cent of that intelligence develops in the first three years of life, another thirty develops in the next five years and the remaining twenty per cent develops between the years of eight and seventeen.

Outline of development

An outline of development does not describe real people as do case studies, but it serves as a guide in our understanding of people and suggests appropriate educational approaches.

Up to the age of five years the home is the dominant factor in the experience of a child; most of what he learns he learns at home. A well-balanced and loving home will give a child a profound sense of security which will help him to develop a sense of self-worth and trust. A sense of security sets him free to explore and adventure. In the first years a child learns basic skills, the boundaries of what is his and not his and he begins to learn to share. In most homes he discovers what it is to be teased and probably thereby discovers the emotions of irritation and perhaps anger; in any case he is likely to experience anger through frustration and to experiment with the use of force as a way of asserting his will. In short, these are years when a child develops a basic trust, achieves a sense of autonomy and goes on to acquire initiative.

Up to the age of five years a child has no grasp of abstract concepts; he cannot link concepts. Therefore he cannot handle a parable, or relate the life of Jesus to the close society in which he lives. But he can experience abstract concepts when a community interprets them for him: he does not say of his home, 'Ah, now I have a feeling of security which is built on the love of my parents', nor does he say of his church, 'Ah, now the love of this community is interpreting to me the love of God in Christ'. In each case, however, those words might represent his inner experience. Already in these first years the child begins to answer the fundamental questions: Who am I? Who are you? What is the world like?

The years five to ten have been described as the years of industry. In these years further skills are developed, say in the use of tools or the playing of an instrument and through social contacts. Play becomes more social. The five to ten year old child plays *with* others whereas younger children play *alongside* others. In these years, children can learn to lose without being saddened and make the more significant discovery that co-operation is more important than losing or winning. A growing sense of selfhood enables him to relate to others and to establish a sustained relationship. During these years the family diminishes somewhat in importance or, at least, others gain in influence. Any adult group outside the home which will accept a child for his own sake and give him a sense of freedom with security has gone a long way towards winning that child to itself.

Between the years of five and ten the child thinks in concrete terms. Numbers fascinate and he may develop an interest in many subjects which have in common that they are concrete or factual, such as stamp collecting, wild animals, the ancient past, fossils, radio or motor cars. At the beginning of this period in life, his thought is related always to himself, but as time goes on this is less so. Piaget says that, 'At about the age of seven the child becomes capable of co-operation because he no longer confuses his own point of view with that of others'.[8] He develops a sense of community and of justice and an interest in world affairs. These are crucial years for the developing of a sense of international citizenship; television, particularly television news, is important in this respect. A child may seem to be full of contradictions as he swings from being self-confident to showing his lack of confidence; he will be egotistic, exploitative and intolerant and also compassionate, generous and helpful. Language and reading are of crucial importance and confer the power of conquest, release and freedom. Stories often relate to attitudes a child learns through playing games. Imagination enables a child to live in a world beyond his own world and to create the world as he would like it to be. He becomes curious about the mystery of death.

Anything that is said about an eleven or twelve year old child may be untrue of a particular individual. One child may develop rapidly and become unmistakably an adolescent young person, another might remain very much a child. It is largely because of the staggering differences between children in these years and because of the contrasting tiredness and vigour, lethargy and excitement which development brings, that most church workers find this age group the most difficult.

Children in the twelfth and thirteenth years are pre-adolescents. Their reading and language ability are highly developed and so is their ability to relate to people. Young people of this age begin to think abstractly and are able to generalize meaningfully. A global perspective can be further developed. They begin to understand the role of language in the creation of culture and to develop a sense of history and tradition, and a world view. Historical explanations can be given in answer to questions about why things are done in particular ways. Material from other parts of the world should be used where it is appropriate, as often as possible. Children of this age can be very introverted or self-reflective; mood music and poetry expressing deep feeling are often appreciated. Rules are no longer absolute, rather they require the agreement of the group and form a social contract. There are in general no unquestionable absolutes, though there may be rules or attitudes which a particular child is not yet ready to question.

Eleven and twelve year olds are able to think of prayer as being communication between persons and to have an awareness of being members one of another. They show compassion and a keen sense of justice. Moral issues are still seen as having a clearly black or white simplicity; there are no shades of grey. Their views, therefore, are often provocative. Eleven and twelve year olds are able to embrace a cause, such as Christian Aid or the mission of the church, with understanding and vigour and are not, as is often the case with older people, afraid of commitment, though in the nature of the case their commitment may be short-term.

Possibly more has been written about adolescence than of any other period of human development; it has fascinated, irritated, lurked in the memory of writers and artists, as well as excited the curiosity of researchers. Adolescents are self-conscious beings who are coming to terms with themselves and with their new powers, their physical strength, sexuality, emotions, intellectual ability and the choices they have to make. A developing sense of selfhood causes adolescents to question all that has formed them through the preceding years, hence they sometimes come into conflict with parents and leaders. Within the church community they are often an irritant, though an important one, since the life of the institution and the foundation of its beliefs should be challenged and re-thought.

Adolescents are capable of principled thought; they can work with and conjecture from a hypothesis. Piaget describes adolescence as the 'metaphysical age *par excellence*; the self is strong enough to reconstruct the universe and big enough to incorporate it'. 'Formal operations provide thinking with an entirely new ability that detaches and liberates thinking from concrete reality and permits it to build its own reflections and theories. With the advent of formal intelligence, thinking takes wings.'[8] Most often adolescents are realists rather than idealists, but seeing the world as it is they are capable of having a vision of the world as it might be and of working for its achievement. In thinking about the world they are able to be, more dispassionate than is usually the case with adults who' are anxious about the ways in which world affairs, and their attitudes to the world, affect the life and security of their families. Above all, adolescents need sensitive adults with whom to work and to serve, to think and to reflect, as equals and colleagues.

The developmental tasks of the years of childhood and adolescence must be achieved before adulthood. When this does not happen time must be spent in adulthood catching up on lost experience, if that is possible. Adults continue to develop a sense of appreciation of life and of the creativity of others; personal relationships deepen. They are able to perceive more of the relationships between ideas and of what influences, determines or changes attitudes. Adults often fear for others and fear generally becomes much more noticeable as an aspect of emotional and rational life. Most adults are concerned with tasks which life has offered or imposed on them; in executing them there is a tendency towards cautiousness. It should not be supposed that adults necessarily have a greater facility with language or that they learn things in ways which are different from those in which a child learns. Most decisions are not based on rational and logical considerations but on feelings and hunches. At their best these contain a distillation of past experience. The liberation of adolescence to which the quotation from Piaget drew attention, is often short lived. Most adults accept that others are in charge. It is, therefore, all the more difficult for adults to respond to the Christian invitation to take part in creating the future. The mystery of death is often forgotten but always returns to tease thoughtful adults. Because traditionally there has been an emphasis on learning in childhood, many adults find it difficult to admit that they are learners, to share their fears and questions and to trust themselves in their weakness to others. The myth of adulthood makes them fear their own vulnerability.

Working with people will enable the reader to know, through experience, that these dry bones live!

It may be argued that in so closely following the work of psychologists this chapter weakens the argument of Chapter

2. On the contrary, I wish to insist that the church community must take personal development seriously as much as individuals must take seriously the ministry of the community. To neglect either means that neither can grow to maturity. Both are needed and both need the liberation of maturity.

Chapter 4

Clarifying Our Aims

In Chapter 1 I said the task of the church 'is to communicate such a vision of life, faith and the world as will fascinate the child (or person of any age) enough to win his allegiance or incite enough curiosity as to suggest it might be worthwhile sticking with it . . . an aim of the church will be to give the child an experience of faith'. From this overall aim of the church community we must now ask: What is the aim of the church's explicit teaching programme? Since it may be some time since those involved in Christian education in a particular congregation clarified their aims, we shall discuss first a number of commonly expressed aims.

Guardians of the church's future

Teachers in church often aim to be the guardians of the church's future. This approach is based on the contention that children must be taught the inherited faith because 'the children of today are the church of tomorrow'. A church worker who loves and is loved by the community of faith will quite naturally want to ensure its future. He may even argue that he wants others, as he has himself, to benefit from a good experience of Christian teaching. There are two reasons why this approach to education must be rejected. In the first place it is a half-truth to say that children are the church of tomorrow. Children are part of the church of today. Those who have been baptised into the community of faith are part of the community equal with persons of any age. Incorporation into the body of Christ should not be confused with ability to share in the government of the church. The church of tomorrow depends upon the adults of today; it is they who make the decisions and, in human terms, determine the church's life, work and witness. In the second place, a person who is strongly motivated by a conscious or subconscious desire to preserve the institution is unlikely to be able to accept children and young people as they are and for their own sakes. Their potential assumes too great an importance. They are noted as, say, potential organists, treasurers, scout leaders or helpers in one way or another. The leader is likely to be too committed to his own hopes to be able to give the child or youth the freedom he needs to develop and to respond to life and to Christ in his own way. Such a response may include rejecting – be it only temporary or partial – a particular institution, belief in Jesus, or his own and his family's history and identity.

On the other hand, a desire to ensure the future of the community is proper. It has biblical warrant, 'one generation shall praise thy works to another'. Leaders must therefore both recognize the rightness and strength of their concern about the church and give due consideration to the freedom of the individual. They must recognize that nurturing children into their heritage is only one aspect of their task, and at times only a minor aspect. A child's freedom, and right to choose, also should be safeguarded in and by the community of faith.

Teaching the Bible

Many people express the aim of church education programmes as being that of helping children to know the stories of the Bible and the biblical revelation. Many who adopt this attitude fail to take account of the wider world. For this reason I call this the ostrich approach: teaching the Bible can be comfortable sand! It has been observed that in Britain the generation now living which knows or has known the Bible best is sixty plus years of age. It is reasonable to ask if this has led to that generation being more notable than younger generations for its Christian insights and prophetic Christian leadership. Many people who are not Christians know the biblical stories; some have an advanced technical knowledge of biblical literature. The plain fact is that knowing the Bible is not enough. Not until we have become part of its story, share its experience and can handle the biblical experience for our own times, does the Bible transform experience. This process is much more subtle than the mere learning of a book of books. I shall return to a discussion of the place and use of the Bible in church education programmes in Chapter 5.

Nurture

The gardening metaphor is used to describe the most popular aim of Christian education. It is used by workers who believe their task is to nurture the tender plant of childhood so that the child will grow up to his full potential. He will become himself. There is much to commend this view. Loving care is decisive in the development of children. We covet for children an experience of a caring Christian community, but the nurture of the community is not enough. Human nature makes it impossible for us to presume that simply because he has been given the opportunity to develop his own personality a child will in fact fulfil his potential as a child of God and enjoy wholeness of life. Indeed loving nurture could pander to a child's innate selfishness.

The major weakness of nurture alone, as I argued in Chapter 1, is that it neglects the critical, reflective and experimental aspects of education. Moreover, we can fulfil ourselves as Christians only to the extent that we come to terms creatively with the society in which we live. The command, 'love your neighbour', must of course be understood personally, and since Christians never know most of their neighbours, it must be expressed also in the kind of society for which Christians work and hope. Social and institutional structures have a place in fulfilling the command to love. A child needs more than an experience of nurture in a Christian community if he is to be equipped to take a constructive part in the re-shaping of society. Christian nurture is inadequate without education related to the social and political realities of life.

Committing information to memory

A minority of church workers still think of children as empty vessels waiting to be filled. They make it their aim to funnel information into children in the belief that one day it will be useful. They hope that the child will be able to draw on what he has learned. This view is often quoted in defence of asking children to learn passages of the Bible by heart.

Underlying this approach are two questionable views. First, that a child can recall with meaning information he has learned by heart without understanding it, and second, that education equals committing of things to memory. I would prefer to say that for people of all ages education involves an exploration of meaning. Information has to be used before it becomes a part of a person's experience. It is more important to use the Bible than to know it by heart. There is little point in cramming information into a child's memory if he does not know how to use it or if the information is not discovered within a meaningful experience. I recollect learning algebraic equations by rote but, since I have never known how to use them, they have gradually been forgotten. When I knew them, they were not given the value of being a working tool. Many people would say something similar about their learning of the Bible or a liturgy. It is of course important that in a proper context children and adults should be helped to build up their personal store of knowledge and information.

Evangelism
Many church workers see their task as being essentially evangelical. Their aim is to conquer the evil of resistance in a child or youth and win him for Christ. Since all Christians live under the command to make disciples of all nations it is difficult to object to this aim, yet a partial objection must be made, perhaps more to the manner in which it is commonly executed, than to the aim itself. There are two major problems: to do with decision-making in education and indoctrination.

Once a leader has decided that evangelism is his aim, it is difficult for him to allow a child freedom in enquiry, to handle material critically, and to avoid at some point putting pressure on a child for a decision. Of course, pressure for a decision can sometimes be wholly – educationally – proper. Until a child has made decisions about, say, aspects of personal relationships or the way in which to weigh and handle evidence, a particular educational exercise may have little validity. The child's development is held up. But these are short-term, immediate decisions. A leader with an evangelical aim is looking rather for a long-term and comprehensive commitment. In fact there might be times in the nurturing of a youth, when it is appropriate to help him in the making of long-term decisions. Some children want to commit themselves as part of their response to Jesus, and when this happens the church community has to find ways of acknowledging their response and commitment in a manner which leaves the child free to develop commitment or to grow out of it. If, for instance, as part of his expression of commitment a child were to become a confirmed member of the church, the nurturing processes of the community should support him in his membership, while in the educational processes he should be encouraged, from his position of commitment and security, to go on exploring, questioning and developing in his own way. This will keep open the risk of his going back on his commitment in confirmation; it is a risk which must be taken for the sake of the child or youth and for the educational integrity of the church.

In Chapter 3 I drew attention to some of the traits of adolescence. In such phrases as 'adolescents . . . are capable of having a vision of the world as it might be and of working for its achievement', I pointed to adolescents' capacity for commitment. Such evidence as I am able to assemble by enquiry in many churches suggests that however open and exploratory has been the attitude of their church, adolescents go through a period of being remarkably single-minded. This single-mindedness may be expressed in a variety of ways: narrow evangelical commitment; work for charities such as Christian Aid or Help the Aged; participation in a Folk Group; social service. It may be the case that churches have to learn how to provide for what might be described as the evangelical phase in the young person's understanding of faith and commitment. Such a phase seems for many young people to be a necessary stepping-stone in the development from childhood through adolescence to a wider and more mature adult commitment.

The decline in the numbers of children attending church has sometimes caused church members to ask how the churches should approach children who have no church connection. I believe that the approach of open-ended educational programmes and social involvement – both including people of all ages – offers appropriate methodologies for welcoming and working with children who have no church connection. Junior clubs, school holiday play facilities and uniformed organizations offer the church opportunities to involve children in the even richer community experience of worship, caring and service. These contain the significant experience for or against which a choice can be made.

Traditionally, Christians have believed that the pursuit of truth is a self-justifying activity and that truth is its own witness. It is not very easy for an evangelist to be so open-minded about explorations into truth. He is fired with a zeal to persuade and convince and does not usually welcome such propositions as those which suggest that he may be wrong or that what he says may be only partially true. Christians who primarily want to add converts to their number are always in danger of lowering their educational standards and of attempting to 'impose' truth as they understand it on the young. Of course, there is inevitably an element of imposition. Every institution makes assumptions which are expressed by its very presence, life-style and unspoken priorities. To ensure their effect is benign, churches must be careful both in their choice and use of educational methods. They must be persistently self-critical about their own institutional life. In their teaching programmes nothing will be safe or sacred, everything (though not everything at one time or the result will be madness) will be open to question. Education sets people free; indoctrination, that is, teaching which implies there is only one viewpoint from which the truth can be seen, enslaves.

Educational methods and techniques are tools which may be used by the evangelist. Education may often fulfil an evangelical role for as people are caught up in an educational process they may be convinced of a truth and commit themselves to it. But the distinction between the educator and the evangelist must remain clear.

Objective opportunity

Uncommitted parents sometimes (less frequently now than hitherto) try to impose an aim on the teaching of children in church. It is based on the view that Christianity and its religious and secular alternatives can be taught objectively; information about them can be piled into the child's memory against the day when in adolescence or adulthood a person can compose his own mind and choose between the various alternatives. This view is based on two serious misconceptions: first, that the church should try to teach a way of life objectively. The church's task is to involve a child in an experience which is all of a piece with what he is taught. If later he rejects his experience and Christianity, he does so, so to speak, from the inside. Further, it must be questioned in what ways a view of Christianity that was susceptible to objective handling would be valid. Such teaching about Christianity would not involve young people in anything like a comprehensive experience of the community of faith. The adolescent or adult would seem, therefore, at best to be basing his choosing on no more than an intellectual shell. The real discovery, rejection or acceptance would be unmade. This, in passing, remains one of the unresolved problems of Religious Studies in day schools. The development of the subject into a study of world religions and cultures offers a child an important opportunity to understand his neighbours and to appreciate others' customs and habits. Religious Education should contribute to good community relations and the creation of a harmonious plural society. But to the extent that such teaching is devoid of real faith experience, it does not constitute an opportunity to discover the inner meaning of any one way of life. Nor, incidentally, does it offer criteria for choosing between them.

Jesus the teacher

That Jesus was addressed as teacher and appears to have accepted that title, is enough to cause some to believe that they are involved in church education simply because Jesus was a teacher. Their aim is to emulate Jesus. It would have been surprising if in the society of his day, Jesus had not been called 'teacher', but those who gave him that title had something more significant in mind than most church leaders can properly claim for themselves. There may be not a little presumption in supposing that church workers are imitating Jesus. In any case, we must ask if the style and methods that were appropriate two thousand years ago are appropriate now across the cultural and social gaps those years represent.

It is more appropriate to affirm that Jesus is supremely the teacher of Christians and of the Church. In the glimpses of his life we see in the Gospels, we find our stance as people and as educators. Jesus offered the disciples through the experience of accompanying him, the opportunity to discover for themselves in activity and reflection. Christian educators may in consequence wish to ask the church, 'How have you enabled people to discover for themselves?' 'How have you enabled people to reflect on experience?' 'How have you enabled people to think in a Christian way about life?' 'In what ways have you invited people to discover for themselves by sharing diverse kinds of Christian colleagueship?'

Aims of church education programmes

In these aims, none of which is wholly satisfactory, we have glimpsed the confused tradition of church teaching. The aims of church education programmes must be consistent with our theological understanding as well as have proper educational validity. Respect should be shown both implicitly and explicitly for the integrity, freedom, and decision-making rights of the learner and for the varied capacities for learning of people of different ages. It must be evident that the teacher is also a learner, and that for both learners and teachers the community of faith is of special importance.

I would express the aims of the church's teaching programme: To help a person to respond to Jesus and to life and to discover with others the meaning of his response for himself and for society; and, in the broadest terms, to prepare a person or a community for worship.

Implications

Implicit in these aims is a dynamic view of Christian faith and life which gives believers a way of seeing, of hearing, of knowing and of responding to life. The Christian has both arrived and is in the process of becoming; he awaits the kingdom and lives in it; he is secure, yet free; he is grounded in tradition, yet a revolutionary. The life in process is dynamic. God is always giving us a new future, but since no one can enter that future alone the challenge to society and of society must be faced.

Unless experience is shared as part of the process of thinking together about the meaning of faith, it is difficult to see how Christian faith can be related to the decision-making of daily life and to the formulation of attitudes. The need for sharing experience and insight puts a considerable demand on the Christian community. Formal life is always easier to manage than informality.

The clues in the Christian faith about meaning and purpose and the message of the saving and liberating love of God should not be handled in such a way as to enchain a person. The portrait of Jesus in the Gospels is of a man who sets others free, and enables them to respond to life. He releases them from the chains of sin and narrowness of outlook; in short, he gives people a new future. Restoration to full health, freedom from crippling conscience or perception of a new religious insight were stepping-stones on the way. New life meant that people were free again to make decisions for themselves. This way of working with people, difficult in the extreme for followers of Jesus who believe they possess and are possessed by truth, must be a goal of in-church workers.

Such an emphasis on helping people to be free to make their own decisions determines our understanding of the place of the 'body' of Christian knowledge – Bible narrative, theology, Church history – in the church's teaching programme. This body of knowledge can be best described as reflection on experience, part of the conversation of the Christian community across the ages and around the world. The conversation has been dynamic and through listening to it succeeding generations have learned the ways of God and men. The Bible, Church history, formulations of the faith and insights into the nature of God and men are part of each generation's gift to the next. The degree to which authority is attributed will inevitably vary from time to time and from person to person. This view will be heard with scepticism by some theologians whose views of the authority of biblical revelation and the Church have sometimes made them less perceptive about human experience; educationalists have been, in general, less dominated by dogmatic considerations.

These few observations on the aims I suggested for a church teaching programme are no substitute for a thorough discussion of aims in the local church. I believe that the emphasis on helping persons to respond to Jesus and to life and working out its meaning for personal and social life leads us also to take cognisance of the enquiry method of learning and of the place of political issues, Christian spirituality, loving relationships, the future and Christian teaching about our ultimate goal, in church education.

The enquiry method

The enquiry method of teaching and learning has been advocated provocatively and well in *Teaching as a subversive activity* by Postman and Weingartner.[12] From this I deduce that teaching and learning in church must be based on the real questions individuals are facing or asking. Though a scheme of education which begins with actual questions is unlikely to lead to a systematic exploration of all the major themes of Christian doctrine and history, it should not be beyond the wit of leaders to compile a check-list and so to discover at the end of any given period which of the major themes of past experience have been neglected. If the omission is significant ways can be found of remedying it.

Political issues

The policies and ambiguities of local, national and international politics have a place in the church's education programme. In the Old Testament the term 'people of God' has particular religious and political connotations embracing the Israelites' consciousness of being a nation state. In the early Christian Church 'people of God' continued to have political significance; the church community stood over against the state. It is of the nature of being God's people that Christians will want to commit themselves politically; love requires it of them. Many of those who attended the final conference on the World Council of Christian Education in Latin America in 1971 were surprised by the extent to which the experience enabled them to see the political significance of their own churches. As they saw the failure of the majority of Latin America's Roman Catholic and Protestant churches to face the terrible problems of housing, land reform, un- and under-employment and were appalled by it, they began to perceive the comparable failure of their own churches. Unless Christian education leads to critical social awareness and responsible social behaviour – involvement in social or political affairs, realistic concern for the poor, hungry, voiceless and powerless – it is failing in part of its *raison d'être*. This does not mean that all church education should concentrate on the high level issues of world affairs. Nor conversely should Christians become interested only in community politics. It is important that each local congregation is informed and enabled to respond at levels which are appropriate to it. There are no hints here of the suggestions that Christians can answer every question or that there are Christian answers to every question. Sometimes it is most important to help a church to recognize that though an issue can be explored, answers to the questions it raises cannot be given. Sometimes a church must be helped to live with the fact that what Christians have to say does not differ from what is said by other sensitive and humanitarian people. And this offers scope for co-operation.

Loving relationships
It is an extraordinary fact that the church which proclaims the message of love spends little time or money helping its members in the practical exercise of love. For instance, few Christian fellowships can cope creatively with tension or disagreements. Though congregations sing hymns about the loving fellowship, loving relationships are not expressed in symbolic acts, except sometimes in the handshake. The lay-out of many churches makes it impossible for those gathering for the major meeting of the church on Sunday to speak to each other. Very often the majority of the congregation knows the names and interests of none of the children or young people. Where this is the case, it is difficult to see the integrity between the sung word and the life of the community. We may surmise that children and young people who leave also find it difficult. Loving relationships are the proper answer to the charge of hypocrisy. A consideration of the nature and quality of the relationships in the Christian

community should find a place in the educational programme of the church.

In addition to this general consideration of relationships, there are specific problems which might be explored. Where this is well done new understanding can lead to new personal development. In one church, for instance, adolescent children and their parents explored together difficulties in their relationships. In another, three generations living in one house talked together, where others could overhear, about the problems and benefits of such an arrangement. Some churches have invited social workers to talk about or to explore in discussion aspects of relationships. A few churches are beginning to understand more about human groups and inter-group relationships. Perhaps the majority of churches have still to learn to distinguish between love as a way of responding verbally to the person of Jesus, and loving as an expression of that response.

Christian spirituality

An understanding of Christian spirituality should undergird the church's teaching. In recent years confidence has declined and there is confusion about how Christians should pray. There have been diversions such as varieties of pentecostalism and transcendental meditation which have attracted some Christians. An exploration of Christian spirituality could lead to a new appreciation of the riches of the Christian history of devotion and, even more, to a reappraisal of the Gospel portrait of Jesus.

Written by people whose purpose was to communicate their faith in Jesus, the Gospels none-the-less offer significant glimpses of his everyday humanity. We see Jesus taking the needs of people seriously and responding to them in ways which make all he said about loving one's neighbour authentic. Through his responses to people and through his teaching, he gave a new future to men and women: the blind were healed, those broken by life were liberated, the crippled were enabled to walk and the courses of more than the lives of the disciples were changed. Through his teaching he roused the imagination of his hearers as much as their intellects and thereby enabled them to discover more of life's and their own potential. So his earliest followers claimed he gave them life.

Erik Routley used the word 'trajectory' in relation to the parables of Jesus. He argues the importance of communications which enable the hearers to receive what is said at their own level of understanding.

The Gospels do not show a man given to speaking in tongues or to Eastern meditation. Rather, we glimpse a man in the midst of hectic life loving his neighbour, speaking his deepest feelings and reflecting on his life and work in communion with a God he knew as Father. Christian spirituality is rooted in this portrait of Jesus in the Gospels. From here we may discover confidence to take seriously conversation with a Father, the unity of the sacred and the secular as it was expressed in incarnation, and God's gifts of faith, hope and love.

The future

Church education programmes should also be concerned with the future; that is part of discovering the meaning of our response to Jesus. Harvey Cox and Jürgen Moltmann have argued that Christians, by definition, will help to shape, rather than wait passively to receive, their future. In *On not leaving it to the snake*, Cox amusingly suggests that the sin of Adam was not that of eating the apple, not that is to say, one of pride, but one of sloth. He gave over his future to others – a woman and a snake. The person of faith will not hand over his future. In *Hope and Planning*, Jürgen Moltmann writes, 'Hope and planning represent the future in different ways; they live with each other and for each other. Unless hope is aroused and is alive, there can be no stimulation for planning. Without specific goals to which hope is directed, there can be no decision about the possibilities of planning; but without planning, there can be no realistic hope. Both hope and planning have their foundation in suffering and in dissatisfaction with the present . . . both find, in new possibilities, ways leading towards another future'.[13] A future described as the Kingdom, affects our political and personal life now. But what kind of future? Pierre Furter has a nice phrase, 'the present itself (must be) given a form which makes possible the eruption of the future'. Is the future, for the Christian, found in the logical projections of the futurologists or is it much more that which is created in the imagination? There is a fundamental difference between the language of futurology and that of faith. Futurology describes how the future will be, assuming it is built on the way things are now in society. Faith, on the contrary, sees the future as a task. It is imaginative, symbolic thought which overcomes the natural inertia of man and endows him with a new ability constantly to reshape his human universe. The future of which the prophets spoke was not an empirical fact, nor a projection, but an ethical and religious task.[14]

The questions faced by every generation are once again being sharpened by experience, namely, 'How can we all live together on this small planet using its resources responsibly and equitably, and in relationships which express mutual care and social justice?' 'What values need emphasizing if such a way of life is to be achieved and maintained?' 'How should technology be deployed?' 'How shall a balance of remunerated work, social wage, and fulfilment through creative leisure and community life, be maintained?' Such questions are not a luxury. They are posed by the experience of every unemployed person, redundant worker, wage claimant and hungry child – and there are more hungry children in the world now than there were ten years ago. These questions directly relate to many familiar social problems and, inevitably, to Christian theology.

The world development movement grapples with the same problems when it asks questions about the meaning of development. Does development, for instance, mean that under-developed countries (as we say) will follow the patterns of the West in acquiring more material possessions, accelerating the pace of life, creating problems of industrial pollution, destroying the environment and over-using natural resources? Could this imaginatively be called 'development'? Perhaps it will be Christians and others in some of the nations which at present are called under-developed who will help us to adopt a much more creative view of development which will be more sensitive both to human personality and to the natural world than anything the West is at present offering them.

But we must face up to our own responsibilities.

The creation of the future is a political task which will have to be undertaken in the harsh realities of the political world. It is also a prophetic task; Christians must show they are not afraid of the vested interests of the *status quo* nor of the evil in man. In helping to clarify the issues and in motivating action Church education has a vital role to play.

Ultimate hope and goal

Related to the Christian's concern for the future is teaching about the ultimate meaning and purpose of life; the word used to describe such teaching is 'eschatology'. Some of the most socially aware people in Western society are those who find their eschatology in pop and folk songs. In many of these, there is an implied downgrading of the importance of technological development and a clear sense of the ultimate victory of love, of the gentler emotions, of peace and of those who work to preserve the environment.

Eschatology is a buttress of any living religion. Christians must know, or have some clues about, the ultimate hope contained in their belief; they must have some sense of the will of God and that he reigns. The biblical phrase, 'the day of the Lord', is sometimes trivialized by being applied to a narrowly ecclesiastical or denominational event. Its proper context is the triumph of God, the transformation of the human scene, the sense of the universality of worship and the holiness in which the secular is taken up into the sacred. Dr. H. Cunliffe Jones expressed this in his essay in *Christian Confidence*. 'The Christian conviction is that in God's final kingdom the long struggle of the historical process will find a satisfying outcome in which the corporate life of mankind will be given a new aliveness to God. God will vindicate both his purpose in history and the meaningfulness of the call he has given to humanity in its total history . . . However precious God's dealings with individuals might be, they are within the corporate reality of mankind, in which God in Christ, the head of all humanity, transforms and brings to triumphant completion its essential life.'[15]

Aims, emphases and gift

In this chapter we have discussed the aims of teaching Christian faith in church. I have mentioned some of the emphases that I would like to see in Church education programmes consequent on the adoption of the aim I have suggested. These include focusing on the actual questions people are asking, giving attention to political matters, thinking about loving relationships, Christian spirituality, concerning ourselves with the creation of the future and with our ultimate purpose and goal.

I have not discussed the teaching of the faith as it is expressed in the traditional statements of the church, say, in the Apostles' or Nicene Creeds. Little of the traditional language of Christianity has been used. Rather, I have approached the teaching of the faith from the standpoint of a person who must discover for himself the experience and conviction to which the traditional statements point. It may be suggested that Jesus himself seems not to have used much religious language. As far as we know, he did not speak of atonement, redemption, saviourhood, lordship, grace and so on. These are the words which faith wants to use of Jesus. They express experience, but are they themselves the essence of the matter? We have to discover the essence of the matter – the truth of God and of the life, purpose and hope he has given to us – for ourselves, and perhaps many times in a lifetime. The language we use to express our faith, trust and hope will embody our gift to the next generation.

Chapter 5

The Use of the Bible in Church Teaching Programmes

Christians are people of the Book. Its story is a part of their story and their story is a part of its story. The Bible is bound to have a very important place in Christian education. Indeed many people believe that though experience might provide a way into the practical task of teaching, the real beginning point of Christian education and worship is the Bible.

Knowing the Bible

The Bible is a decisive part of the living Christian tradition. Without its record of experience the keystone of tradition would be missing. Within the Christian Church there is a historical continuity of which sense can be made only by reference to the Bible. It is a Christian's main point of reference, source of confidence and of insight. A believer is impoverished who does not know the source of the Christian tradition, its early stumblings and joyful affirmations. He needs to feel that he is part of the pilgrim people of faith whose life and thought is interpreted by the New Testament, which is itself interpreted by the life of the pilgrim people now. The Bible and the living tradition of the Church interpret each other.

Arguing in wider terms, some have said that no one in the Western world can be said to be educated unless he knows the Bible well enough to understand references to it and quotations from it in literature, the law and other parts of academic and institutional life. Whether this is a reason for teaching the Bible in church or for asserting its place in a liberal state education, or both, is a matter for discussion. What is not open to argument is that the Bible is a part of the currency of Christian thought. No one can progress far in talking about Jesus or any of the great Christian themes without reference to it. It is a major resource for anyone who tries to think theologically about life in the world now. For instance, a deeper knowledge of the Bible might enlighten discussion in some local churches about the Christian Church's involvement in politics; such a knowledge might also help Christians to hold together the sacred and the secular and to find in such a union a deep sense of renewal and dynamic purpose.

One practical educational reason for insisting that Christians should know their Bible, is that without this knowledge so many discussions have to begin further back than they should; time has to be wasted while basic work is undertaken. Some people who are thinking at graduate level in other subjects are still at primary level in the Christian faith because they do not know the Bible nor how to handle it. The church worker, at least at adolescent and adult levels, should be able to take a basic knowledge of the Bible for granted. But before we can discuss how this knowledge might be acquired or how the Bible might be used in Church education, we must recognize some of the difficulties the Bible presents to our contemporaries and to children in particular.

Facing some difficulties: A sense of time

Few children of pre-adolescent years can grasp the vast time span within the Bible. In an introductory course on the Bible, junior age children might learn that the writing, re-writing and formulation of the Old Testament took some eight hundred years and that of the New Testament some three hundred years, but the implications of this information are largely beyond their grasp. Young children cannot comprehend the broad sweep of history. The cultural, social and theological developments during a period of eleven hundred years which in turn lead to changes in the meanings of words, mean little to them. And not young children only. A sense of time or history seems to parallel, in personal development, the ability to conceptualize.

In addition to the 'internal' problem of time, there is the 'external' problem of the span between biblical times and contemporary life. Most pre-adolescent children live with the contradiction of treating the stories and morals of the

Bible as though they were contemporary, while knowing they come from long ago. Most are unable to understand that the Bible is a collection of statements of faith intended to be reliable only in this respect: it shares the faith of the community out of which it grew. The pre-eminent function of the biblical record is to help us to have faith. Because it is such a book of experience and faith Christians treasure it. But the leap over the centuries from one complex of cultures and understandings of people and of the universe to another suggests that we ought not to give the impression that the message of every part of the Bible can be applied directly in modern life. This danger is seen more clearly when in thinking about a life-theme or life-issue we are asked to explain 'What the Bible says'. It may say nothing or a number of conflicting things. The process of thinking in a Christian way about life-themes requires a more subtle approach.

Different kinds of literature

One of the advantages of modern versions of the Bible is that they are printed to show clearly the difference between poetry and prose. But poetry is only one of the many kinds of literature in the Bible; typography does not distinguish between history, biography, theological reflection, prophecy, apocalyptic, parable, story, myth or law, nor can it distinguish between first-hand accounts, diverse traditions and editorial comment. This variety of literature poses problems for some adults and adolescents as well as for pre-adolescent children. And the concepts they are used to communicate constitute a further problem.

Adult experience and hope

The Bible is a book of adult experience and aspiration. Whenever it is used with children or adults, care must be taken not to trivialize the experience to which it refers. For instance, though experience of parents' love is one of the ways in which a child is enabled to give meaning to the word 'love' when it is used of God, we cannot equate the universal, forgiving and creative love of God in Christ with the love parents give their children. Nor in talking to young children can the friendship of which Jesus speaks in the Gospel of

John chapter 15 be equated with friendship of the lollipop man, though the child's trust of the latter will enable him to understand to some extent the language of trust which is used in relation to Jesus. The work of Ronald Goldman is most pertinent to this point; see again Chapter 1. Generally speaking, I accept Goldman's thesis based on the results of his research into the conceptual ability of children of different ages.[16] The weakness of his work for our purpose is that it took account only of conceptual ability and of day school experience. It took no account of how children learn through emotional, aesthetic or community experience. While church workers would be foolish to neglect Goldman's work, the experience of some of the most able and sensitive of them suggests, as I have said, that in an all age community children are able to grasp the meanings of ideas which would be far beyond them were they only in a peer group. Christian faith and life must not be thought of only in terms of abstract ideas; they are expressed also through atmosphere, service, colour, sound, witness, relationships, drama, mime and worship . . .

In an unpublished thesis on *The incidence of concrete and abstract religious thinking in the interpretation of three Bible stories*, John Peatling's findings generally supported those of Piaget and Goldman.[17] But Peatling found that children developed over a much longer period than Goldman had suggested. In contrast to Goldman's findings that children do not leave the stage of concrete religious thinking until thirteen/fourteen years (mental age) Peatling suggests that, whereas nine year olds think in concrete terms, ten year olds (mental age) were beginning to develop beyond this, though the ability to think abstractly was not reached until sixteen years (mental age). His work also suggests continued development until the age of twenty. Though Peatling suggests that mental age is more important than socio-economic class, nevertheless 62 per cent of the sample of children with whom he worked went to church every week and 64.5 per cent said religion was of some importance in their lives.

Most Christian educators will agree with my outline of some of the problems inherent in using the Bible with children. But there agreement ends.

The Bible as story

The Bible is not a story book. It is, as I said, a book of adult experience and aspiration, though much of this adult experience is expressed in story form. Some parts of the Bible are collections of stories which were part of an oral story-telling tradition for years before they were written down. The texts of such stories as we have them in the Bible cannot be said to be 'correct' or definitive; they are best heard not in sonorous pulpit tones but from the lips of a story-teller who can draw his hearers into the living tradition and experience of the story. But is this likely to happen unless the hearers share or can enter imaginatively into the adult experience of the story and have a knowledge of its context and background? At what age are children likely to be in this position?

Take, for example, the story of Moses being found in the rushes. We do not need to know whether this story is true in the sense that it tells of an actual incident. We hear it as part of the story of Moses and of the deliverance from Egypt. A few people will see in the story universal psychological symbolism. For the majority of those who hear it read in church, it speaks of the saving work of God. Yet many people would tell this story to young children. They would argue that children sing many songs and hear many stories they do not fully understand, such as Ring-a-ring o' Roses and Cinderella. Stories communicate ideas and values, they stimulate the imagination and provoke response; tradition is communicated through the telling. Children who know particular collections of stories have a sense of belonging.

I have no doubt about the importance of story in the educational process or of the strength of the views I have just represented. I wonder if it is possible, however, to distinguish between our use of stories in general and our use of those from the Bible? Keeping the story of Moses' rescue as our example: might not its use with children be governed by the answers given to such questions as: What is my purpose in telling this story? Is the context in which I am telling the story appropriate to the context and meaning of the story as I understand it in the Old Testament? Am I able to tell enough of the story for its meaning and place in the Jewish tradition

to be evident? Are the concepts within the story appropriate
to the age of the children to whom I propose to tell it? These
last two questions raise particular difficulties. Within the
Jewish faith the stories of the Old Testament help to build up
attitudes: a Jewish boy grows to feel himself part of his people.
He not only belongs, he senses the continuity between his
people now and those of long ago. For a Christian, the Old
Testament serves a different purpose. Other questions to be
asked are: Is the telling of this story a substitute for an experience in the community? How will the context in which I am
telling the story help the child to use the story to develop his
own theological thoughts?

In *The Teaching Methods of Jesus*, Douglas Hubery says,
'Jesus clearly regarded the story as one of the best methods
of making known the truths he wanted to impart. Indeed, it
is difficult to imagine how some of his truths could have been
imparted, with so good effect, in any other way'.[18] I agree,
but perhaps one of the dangers of modern versions of the
Bible is that their simple, direct language gives the impression
that the mystery at the heart of the experience has been
removed along with the older language. This may be very
misleading.

The *Little Owl Bible story books* constitute an interesting
case.[19] They comprise exceedingly well written and well illustrated paraphrases of New Testament stories and are intended
for very young children. The language is direct and simple.
One of the best of the series is *The man who helped*, based
on the Gospel of Luke, chapter 10, verses 29–37. With
Hubery we could say of this story that it is difficult to imagine
how its message could have been imparted, with so good
effect, in any other way. But in attempting to make a parable
into a story suitable for young children, the children are
presented with something which, though biblical in spirit, is
significantly different from the original. Young children will
hear the story as a true story (as though it happened in
history) and will not realize that it is a parable, nor would
they understand it if they did. The message of the parable is
somewhat more profound than the moral on the last page,
'be kind and help others'. Indeed, according to Luke, the
parable is told in answer to a question about eternal life. A

New Testament scholar has commented, 'It is clear that Jesus had intentionally chosen an extreme example; by comparing the failure of the ministers of God with the unselfishness of the hated Samaritan, his hearers should be able to measure the absolute and unlimited nature of the duty of love . . . The Law of love called him to be ready at any time to give his life for another's need . . . The value which Jesus sets upon love to the needy and afflicted, comes out in the description of the sentence pronounced at the Last Judgment.'[20]

We need to ask whether it is serving the best interests of the child to tell him a story in childhood knowing that the child will have to re-learn its purpose and meaning later in life. Can a child, of the age for which *The Little Owl Bible story books* are intended, understand the question to which the story is given as an answer? By telling such stories we may unwittingly encourage a child to believe that because he knows a number of stories he knows Christianity. Indeed, some children who have ceased to attend a church between their ninth and twelfth years have had the impression that they have known enough to decide for or against Christianity, whereas all they have known were a few Bible stories. Some church workers would say that there are enough stories and accounts of historic and contemporary incidents to communicate ethos and values and to stir the imagination without treating as story that which is not so much story as a vivid proclamation of faith. Others would say there is no one proper way to hear the stories of the Bible: adults vary in their understanding of the meaning of biblical stories and throughout adult life the significance of the stories changes. If children hear the stories of Jesus they have a foundation on which understanding and faith can be built.

Whatever are our views about using the Bible with either children or adults, we must be careful not to give the impression that the Bible is something which it is not. It is a book of faith, failure and aspiration; above all, it is about the relationship of God and his creation, humankind. We must not trivialize the profoundest human experiences which are its central concern.

Children and the Bible

In view of the difficulties I have outlined, and the discussion I have summarized, some church workers have asked whether the Bible should have any place at all in the education of children. Perhaps, they suggest, this essentially adult book should be kept for the education of adults? Children would not turn to the Bible as a story book if adults did not encourage them to do so! I have no hesitation in saying that some parts of the Bible should be withheld until at least young adulthood and that it must be recognized that some adults will never have more than the haziest notion of the meaning of certain books and passages. This is not a judgment on their ability to respond to God or to live faithful and immensely useful lives: to some children and adults the word of God is communicated principally through the Bible, to others it is communicated principally through experience in the community of faith. Whether it is through the Bible or the Church or through both, our grounds for believing in Jesus, known in history, and our understanding of him known eternally as Christ, must be made clear. We should not minimize the importance of the Bible in Christian experience and learning nor, being aware of how people learn, should we minimize the importance of the church in Christian experience and learning.

Children should hear and use those parts of the Bible which are appropriate to their age. Or to put the matter more precisely, children should be helped to use the parts of the Bible which their past experience enables them to interpret and which interprets their experience.

Perhaps, when we speak of knowing the Bible, a distinction should be made between those who are learners in the faith but uncommitted, and those who are learners in the faith and committed. The former do not usually hear the Bible for its own sake. They explore it, they learn to use it and through using it they may begin to value it. The day might come when experience will give meaning to the language they have heard used to describe the Bible: it may become for them the *Holy* Bible or the Word of Life. The committed on the other hand, will use it both in the way I have just described and, because of their trust of its Gospel, will want to know it for its own sake as well. It is doubtful if it would help the uncommitted learner if we were to insist on his learning the Bible for its own sake; attitudes of faith must be given time to develop.

Are there, then, any general guide-lines for the church worker about using the Bible in Church education? It is possible to accede to the request of many church workers by suggesting lists of the parts of the Bible that are appropriate for each age group. For instance: three, four and five year olds may use verses expressing thankfulness, happiness and praise.

A paraphrased outline of the life of Jesus giving the ethos of his life without attending to detail, e.g., mentioning his birth in humble surroundings and his place in the love of Mary and Joseph. Jesus was one of a family of seven or more children. When he grew up he helped and taught people.

Some healing stories can be used which show Jesus healing because he understood and loved people, rather than because he was a magician. It is important that in paraphrasing the outline of the life of Jesus stories are not invented. Omit all reference to the Easter event.

Five, six and seven year olds: in addition to the foregoing, verses expressing regret for hurting others; stories from the Gospels of ordinary human encounter. Some glimpses of happy human relationships in the letters; some of the 'concrete' aspects of the teaching of Jesus.

Seven and eight year olds: in addition to the foregoing, a paraphrased outline of the story of the people of Israel so as to set Jesus within the context of a worshipping community; verses from the poems of faith.

Eight, nine, ten and eleven year olds: in addition to the foregoing, background information about the creation and content of both Testaments. Introduction to some of the concerns of the letters and to the mission of the early Church. An introduction to biblical criticism and to different kinds of literature. More of the 'concrete' teaching of Jesus. Introduction to some of the characters of the Old Testament. The Easter event.

Eleven, twelve and thirteen year olds: in addition to the foregoing, parables. Those parts of the Old Testament which reflect the turmoil of human development and, therefore, relate to early adolescent experience of, for instance, the search for identity, the questioning of conscience and the search for a purpose of the people of Israel. The Acts of the Apostles. Develop the ability of children of this age to handle the Bible critically and stress the importance of using the Bible.

Thirteen, fourteen and fifteen year olds: in addition to the foregoing, the great ideas of the Old Testament. The major issues of the letters. Those parts of the Gospels not yet used, and the Gospel of John.

Fifteen plus: in addition to the foregoing, the remainder.

This kind of outline is only of the most general use. A much fuller treatment of the subject will be found in Douglas Hubery's *Christian Education and the Bible*.[21] In the main, children should be encouraged to use and enjoy those parts of the Bible which both interpret and are interpreted by their past experience. But we should also remember that as well as confirming, interpreting and illuminating experience, words also arouse curiosity.

A subtle approach allows a leader, or parent, more scope and flexibility. The sensitive leader who knows well the people – children or adults – with whom he is working can sometimes use material about which it would be impossible to make a general recommendation. Experience is the key. Care should always be taken in selecting passages that the language, style and conceptual difficulties of the literature are not beyond the learner's linguistic and conceptual ability.

Life themes

In describing the Bible as a sharing of experience, I must emphasize that I am not looking to the Bible for worked-out schemes of thought – a biblical doctrine of work for instance. Rather, we find in the experience of Israel and the early Church, moments of insight, of imagination, of revelation, of perception and of perspective; moments when the person of faith has expressed his innermost trust, fears and hopes and thus 'shared' his God or his Lord. The Bible shares the

experience of the community of Israel struggling to be a
people of God and of the new Israel trying to work out the
meaning of Jesus, each in the world of their own time. I
would rather not speak of the 'relevance' of the Bible to
contemporary life. I prefer to speak of the Bible offering us
clues about meaning and purpose and signposts of the way. To
speak of relating the Bible to life suggests a dualism between
the word and the world. It implies a dualism between the
Christian and the world. If there is a message to be discovered
in the Bible, we can do no other than discover it in the
context of the world as we know it.

The term 'life-theme' refers to 'teaching by means of
themes, based upon the real life experience of the children . . .
a life-theme can take any area of a child's life, of which he
has first-hand knowledge'.[22] Whether for 'life-theme' we
substitute 'living issues' or 'life experience', the importance
of the phrase, 'of which the child has first-hand knowledge'
must be stressed. We cannot expect the Bible to fit neatly
into every contemporary life-theme. Sometimes there
will be only a general relationship of Gospel and theme. In
using the Bible in the exploration of a life-theme, the message
of the Bible should not be forced, nor should it be neglected.
The Bible should be used as one of the many sources of
experience to which reference may be made. The learner
may then find that experience speaks to experience. Through
using the Bible the learner may begin to respect it and to see
that it is about him and his world. Harold Loukes made the
point which now more appropriately belongs to learning in
church than to learning in school, 'Religious Education
should be conducted in an atmosphere of realism and
relevance . . . the present world as immediately experienced
by our young people, would provide the themes, which
would be pressed back to the Bible where these themes were
originally, and profoundly explored'.[23] As he gets to know
the Bible by using it he will have to face some of its textual
and contextual problems. Thus he will have to learn also
about the Bible.

Hearing the Bible

Much of the foregoing has presupposed that the reader sits in judgment on the Bible to search out its message. The Bible also sits in judgment over us; it addresses us. The Bible contains a 'given' word of experience – of life and hope – through which Christians believe the Holy Spirit can speak.

Anyone who has taken a child to an art gallery knows that it is better to select one picture or one room for inspection rather than try to view the whole gallery. Even so, depending on the age and development of the child, the young person might remark on the splendour of a gilded frame or on a detail in a picture rather than on a grand theme or masterly composition. On the other hand, a child may receive a series of impressions which, though he cannot formulate them verbally, combine to influence not only his appreciation of art, but his personal development. He may enjoy it! Either way, there will be little point in trying to add to the experience by explanations, though it may be useful to clinch the experience by helping the child to reflect on it as much as he is able. The work of art has communicated. Perhaps too few leaders and parents are prepared to allow children to enjoy the Bible; to allow a simple positive sentence from a poem or affirmation, or a longer quotation, speak for itself. Of course, care will be shown in the choice of quotation. The child might not understand it completely but, in any case, it should be chosen so that it will be impossible for a child to understand the passage in a way which is contrary to the intention of the quotation. A child may not understand Raphael's 'The Nymph Galatea' (circa 1514), but if he comes to the conclusion that it is just a silly collection of bodies, when it is generally thought of as remarkable for its form and movement and as a milestone in the development of art, he would be so seriously wrong as to have to unlearn the message he had received, later in life. Raphael's 'The Nymph Galatea' is not suitable for young children, nor are some subtle passages of the Bible. But those that are should be heard.

I would stress again the importance of letting the Bible speak for itself. It has a unique and honoured place in the life of the Christian community. It has been shown in experience to be one of the means through which people are addressed. Its power to address us, combined with our reflection on the human experience it describes, are important parts of our Christian experience and growth.

Chapter 6

Significant Developments

The minister of a London church commented, 'We are fortunate in not having pews', to which another replied, 'We are fortunate in not having a church!' If the Church were beginning again in one of the countries where it has long been established few people would expect it to amass buildings or to take on its present organizational form. In *Christianity at the Centre* John Hick remarked, 'The churches as they now are cannot survive for very long. Nor should we wish to prolong their life beyond the point at which new and more viable forms of Christian life have become apparent. Indeed what is to be feared is rather that the present churches, unadapted to the new age, *will* contrive to survive – but by going culturally underground and becoming totally irrelevant to the on-going life of mankind. In these days when the obsolescence of the church's modes of thought and life is so painfully evident, but while there is still no clear vision of the right ways in a changing world, it is increasingly difficult for Christians acutely aware of the need for new forms to continue within the old'.[24] A church which did not have organization enough to enable consultation and co-operation between groups of believers, or did not have the services of some full-time specialist officers, or could not be reminded of its heritage by a few great historic church buildings, would be singularly impoverished. Conversely a church which is too structured, too dependent on full-time officers and burdened with buildings created for the liturgies of long ago will inevitably find it difficult to be responsive to the age in which it lives. Heritage is both a burden and a boon.

Worship in the round
Some churches are beginning to change both their styles of meetings and their meeting places. An elder wrote, 'If you say you will come to church with me on Sunday morning,

you will have to make a choice. At 10.30 will you go into the
Preaching Service or into Worship in the Round? The
Preaching Service follows the traditional pattern of the
Reformed liturgy. Worship in the Round, meeting in the
church hall, uses a great variety of methods and approaches,
and involves both adults and children of all ages. Both
services are based on the *Partners in Learning* theme for the
day, and last forty-five minutes. At 11.15 the whole church
gathers together to celebrate Holy Communion or to participate in Family Worship which is planned as an appropriate
climax to both the earlier activities.

'This Sunday morning pattern is now in its third year. It
evolved after four years of discussion and of trying other
patterns. In roughly an hour and twenty minutes the congregation has an opportunity to worship and learn in a style of its
choosing, and to converse. The church has maintained its
unity. Because of the considerable movement of people
between the two services there is not a radical and a traditional congregation uneasily sharing family worship together.

'The Preaching Service and the Family Worship are usually
led by the minister. Worship in the Round is led by teams of
volunteers. A team appointed to be responsible for a course
usually starts preparing about six weeks before the first
Sunday of the course. A four week course usually requires
four preparatory meetings. The kind of question a team must
ask is: Given this theme, how can we enter into it and use it
as the springboard for learning and worship? What can we
(children and adults) do together? Are there points at which
it will be necessary for children to work together (and of
what age, and for how long)? What are the most appropriate
methods for us to use in exploring or celebrating this theme?
How does the theme lead into and grow out of worship? . . .
So, if you come into Worship in the Round, you might be
invited to work in a small or large group. There might be
children working as equals with you in the group; you might
be painting, discussing, creating a collage, studying the Bible;
hearing a local councillor, reflecting on an aspect of the life
of the local community, playing a game, listening to an
anthology, thinking radically about world development. . . .
'We have found that we cannot always accommodate the

children with the adults, but when the two are together we have our liveliest sessions. Often children liberate adults; involvement in a natural community enables children to handle concepts much in advance of those they can cope with in peer groups. Adults and children together have a sense of the adventure of faith; both face enormous difficulties in being Christian; both have much to celebrate; both share the church's pastoral and socio-political concerns.

'We are fortunate in that about thirty people are ready to take part in the leadership of Worship in the Round. With so many being involved in leadership and in the making of affirmations and the asking of fundamental questions, the minister's role is changed. He joins in the preparation groups. He is a very important resource person in the group but he does not take a leadership role and his contributions are given the same joyful welcome or critical scrutiny as anyone else's. During one course each year the minister takes part in Worship in the Round and other members of the church lead the Preaching Service.

'On three or four Sundays in the year a Festival Service is planned to enable the whole congregation to worship together throughout.

'Our reflection on this experience leads us to be profoundly grateful for the stimulation of *Partners in Learning*. However much we may on occasion reject its suggestions, its value as a resource and a catalyst is proven. We object to our pattern of worship being described as experimental. We have been doing this too long for that term to be appropriate. We think of ourselves simply as being a company of people trying to find ways which are appropriate to our particular experiences. We are as much concerned to discover what can be meant by our being a church community as what is meant by worship. We do not believe that we have found anything on which we ought to settle permanently. Church life should always be interim – so far so good – and open to new insights, development and growth. We would heartily encourage others to look for ways of enabling people, at the usual times of worship, to make a choice about their style for the day. But we would do so with the warning that the way is not easy; it deeply offends some of those who cherish a traditional liturgy to see their peers appearing to turn their backs on it.'

Community and participation

A church in the North-West reports that its Sunday morning programme begins at 10.15. During the first thirty-five minutes there is group work, the church being divided into three basic groups, the under fives, the six to ten year olds and the young people and adults. The leadership of these groups changes every four to six weeks. At 10.50 everyone joins together for refreshments and conversation. During this time, local community concerns are shared. At 11.15 everyone, except the babies, goes into church for service of worship which ends at noon. A church in East Anglia reports a similar programme except that the order is reversed; the programme begins with worship.

A church in the South-East holds two services each Sunday morning. One is traditional in form; the other for children and adults learning and worshipping together could be described as Worship in the Round. The traditional service still has the larger congregation, while the Worship in the Round attracts young people, a few families and perhaps more adventurous spirits. It is this service which increases in size. Occasionally, a sermon is included in Worship in the Round so that the participants are not deprived of that element of worship.

In a London church the minister prepares an outline for a Sunday morning session about two months in advance. This is duplicated and becomes the basis of a Worship Workshop to which all who are interested are invited. A programme of learning and worship is prepared and leaders are appointed by the Worship Workshop. The programme for each Sunday follows the pattern the Worship Workshop decides is most appropriate to the occasion. This depends on the subject and the style of treatment it proposes. Usually worship and learning are integrated. At different times the congregation may be divided into age groups or family (all age) groups.

In another church the programme is prepared well in advance so that all the meetings of the church can be involved in the worship theme. Thus in any month the worship, the meeting with the parents, the study group, the Women's

Fellowship and the Social Service Group are all linked together by a common theme which is explored in very different ways. The planning for this is undertaken by the Preparation Group to which the leaders of all the church's groups are invited. A duplicated programme is prepared and is a useful 'give-away' for church visitors and the major item of the church's publicity.

In all these churches the courses or services are based on published courses more or less adapted to suit local requirements or on a theme which has arisen in the life of the church. Such a concern could arise because of the special interest of a person or group within the church. It may be an issue which is of national or local significance at the time, such as a new redevelopment plan for the area or town, or the problem of homelessness in the area. Or it may be an aspect of a previous theme which could not be adequately dealt with at that time or which showed up a particular weakness in the church's life and learning. One such self-programmed course for a church community is described in a paper by John P. Reardon, see Appendix B.

It is not always the Free Churches which are in practice freest to explore new expressions of Christian community life and worship. Some of the most adventurous worship I have experienced was led by Roman Catholic priests. Many Anglicans are using the opportunities offered by the Series 3 liturgy very imaginatively; indeed it is likely that there have been more developments in community life and attempts at participative learning and worship in the Church of England than in any other Communion. Often, regrettably, children have been excluded and little time has been allowed for quiet waiting on God.

Church conferences
Church or family days play an important part in the community experience of some churches. These are often one day conferences for the family of the church, beginning perhaps with Sunday morning worship. Experience suggests that more is achieved in one day spent together than in many more ordinary Sunday mornings. Some churches are arranging occasional weekend conferences at a conference centre

or using another church as a centre. In some areas such weekend conferences are arranged ecumenically. In one church it has been agreed that the traditional liturgy and preaching of a sermon shall happen only every four or six weeks so that other forms of community life can be developed on the other Sundays. One small north country town engages all the churches, schools and major organizations of the township in an educational project every other year. The project which usually aims to raise awareness of another part of the world and uses every kind of social and educational method, begins in the autumn and continues until the following May.

In some areas the extra-mural departments of a University, the Workers Educational Association or staff of a College of Education are willing to respond to requests for courses. These are usually, practically and educationally, unadventurous main-stream courses, say, in New or Old Testament background, Church History or Theology. They have sometimes been particularly valuable in helping to equip lay leaders in local churches. Some of the denominational colleges offer a similar facility.

Sharing common concerns

One church arranged occasional one-off or short series of meetings for people in the locality with a common concern. The aim of the meeting was to enable sharing, reflection and mutual encouragement. People involved in such groups have included those preparing for retirement and those having been retired for one year, middle-grade managers, young marrieds, people in particular professions . . . Another church runs a community newspaper and provides the leadership of the local residents' association, and yet others take leading parts in organizing local community festivals.

Week-day or Sunday

The question is being asked in some places whether Sunday is the best day for the church's major meeting. A survey has suggested that families spend sixty per cent of their leisure time visiting relatives. One response to the problem this creates is to meet the children of church families on Sunday and to arrange week-day clubs or a week-day Sunday school for other children. Churches are usually unwilling to move the major meeting for worship to a week-day evening because of the offence this might cause. But it would be much more satisfactory from my point of view if the whole programme of learning and worship were transferred rather than just a part of it. Week-day Sunday school and clubs serving the same purpose are likely to perpetrate a worse division between church and Sunday school than was the case earlier in this century. It deprives the children of parents who do not attend church of the very experience I believe is decisive for their growth and understanding.

At least one town centre church has a week-day church evening: this begins with a buffet meal which is available from five o'clock until six thirty. A frequently changed leadership group plans a programme which includes learning and worship, social and service activities, and meetings through which the business of the church is formally conducted. Children are often present throughout though sometimes there are peer group activities. The programme ends at seven thirty.

Educational impact

The educational impact of the church is not and cannot be limited to those activities which are programmed as educational. The whole life of the church contributes. For example, a person may most experience the educational influence of a church through membership of a choir or a group assembled to decorate an old person's home. Nor is the educational influence of the church the prerogative of those who are recognized within it as teachers or leaders. We will now look at the number of potential or actual developments some of which originate from outside the churches and are obviously concerned with much more than teaching.

Theological workshop

The term 'theological workshop' has already become part of the language of the church. It describes a day or longer conference in which people try to think in a Christian way about a contemporary issue. Sometimes the participants are

engaged in one profession; they may be Christian teachers
trying to think, say, about the values inherent in the way
schools are structured or about the place of Christianity in
the teaching of world religions; they may be doctors discussing contemporary medical dilemmas; or they may be an
inter-disciplinary group having a common interest in, say,
the countryside, or in wrestling with the meaning of worship.
Sometimes theology workshops are very mixed assemblies of
people who have in common a desire to learn how to think in
a Christian way and to discover what counts in the forming of
a Christian view.

A theological workshop often involves only articulate
people, but it need not be so limited an event. People who
do not think of themselves as intellectuals can talk well about
what is important in their lives. An issue can be explored
with the help of drama, role play, or mime and through
conversational reflection consequent upon some form of
corporate action or service. As it is generally used the term
'theological workshop' refers to a specially arranged and self-
conscious attempt to think about an aspect of life using such
clues about purpose and meaning as can be found in the
Christian message. But there is a sense in which the term
should be applicable also to the ordinary week by week life
of the Christian community. The church can be called a
community of faith only if those in it, taking Jesus to be the
corner-stone of their lives, are working out together what
faith in Jesus means. Often they will disagree; sometimes
they will feel compelled to common action. It will be necessary to handle both the major issues of daily news and television documentaries, and the tender issues and difficult
decisions of ordinary personal life. In this I am describing an
adult activity, but one in which it is vital that children and
young people should sometimes take part and often overhear.
The young need to know that Christian life is not only – as
they commonly experience it – hymn-singing, praying and
talking in the formal setting of the church. Christian faith
involves people in coming to grips in the name of Jesus with
the ambiguities, filth, joy and breadth of daily living and in
learning to listen as people who are continually addressed.
The people of the church will remain inhibited and immature

as long as they are dominated by the sermon or the professional ministry.

It is one of the ironies of church life that church people
shrug their shoulders at the mention of the word 'theology'.
Church people have been no more likely than anyone else to
protest when politicians dismiss as 'theology' a topic which in
their view is unimportant or nonsense. The fault lies partly
with some theologians – those who still believe theology is
almost exclusively a historical or academic discipline – from
whom the churches must shake themselves free. Because
people have believed theology was only learning handed
down from the past they have fought shy of it and have
ignored it as though it were irrelevant to life now. It would
be foolish to ignore past experience or to suppose that
importance were to be attributed only to modern achieve-
ments, but fundamental to the arranging of a theological
workshop is the presupposition that theology is a way of
thinking about life. Theologizing is a creative exercise. A. J.
Wesson argued in a paper on *Theology and Community
Development*, 'The task of theology is not to defend and
persuade people to absorb a set of doctrines, but rather to
think theologically, to respond to human experience and to
explore it in the light of the conviction that God has given to
man in Christ the clue to human existence.'[25]

Underlying this approach to theological education is the
questioning of some of the most commonly held assumptions
about education. I want us with E. D. Kelley in *Education
for what is real*[26] at least to question all the following assumptions: that education is the acquisition of knowledge and that
knowledge is something which has existed for a long time
and is handed down on authority; that subject matter taken
on authority is educative in itself; that the best way to set out
subject matter is in unassociated fragments or parcels; that
such a fragment or parcel is the same to the learner as to the
teacher; that education is supplementary to and preparatory
to life, not life itself; that since education is not present
living, it has no social aspects; that the teacher can and should
furnish the purpose/need for the acquiring of knowledge;
that working on tasks devoid of purpose or interest is good
discipline; that the answer to the problem is more important

than the process; and that it is more important to measure what has been learned than it is to learn.

Social projects

It is generally true to say that the more people are involved in the learning process, the more they are able to gain from it. Social and political projects cover a wide range of activity: campaigning about children's play facilities in a housing area; the regular visiting of all the elderly in an area; organizing a panel of interpreters; running a housing association; helping to found and run hostels for the homeless or for people in special need of care; providing facilities for and helping to staff a youth club for young patients in a mental hospital; arranging a fast, or political lobbying to draw attention to Government policy regarding the poorer nations of the world; arranging an old people's luncheon club; organizing a clearing-house for local community service groups. These are a few of the activities that have been undertaken by local churches singly or by Councils of Churches. All have offered opportunities to people in the churches to grow in understanding and compassion. Many more have had a similar experience through being involved in local community organizations. Serious account should be taken of the importance of this kind of learning process which contrasts, because of the emphasis on participation, with the usual methods of communication (and, therefore, learning) in traditional church life. The advice of the Welsh preacher to the young men, 'Tell 'em what you're going to tell 'em, then tell 'em, then tell 'em what you've told 'em', might have been an advance in its day, but it hardly takes account of what we know now of how people learn.

In this context the importance of learning games may be mentioned. This is a developing field. The educational games used in church circles are usually an extended role play, simulation, or a variation of a board game. Involving people in a hypothetical situation which demands responsible decision-making, simulating situations in which they and others have to live and decide responsibly, or setting out a major topic in a play situation, opens new possibilities for learning. Children's board games can sometimes be adapted to introduce ideas or to facilitate common experience.

Family life

Some churches are now devoting a great deal of time to meeting parents. Some are involving parents in their educational programmes. This is all to the good because many parents are suspicious of educational approaches which emphasize the importance of experience. They remain suspicious until they have had an opportunity to learn experientially themselves – or to recognize that that is what they have always been in the habit of doing! It is hardly appropriate to lecture parents on the experiential method. In some churches a leaflet is prepared for the beginning of each series of Sunday sessions. This outlines the course and suggests ways in which parents can contribute to it at home during the weeks ahead. In churches where the educational programme of the whole church is conceived as one enterprise, even though the adults and children may for part of the time meet separately, such a leaflet outlines the activities of the whole church community. Involving parents in the training class for the leaders of children's groups facilitates parent and leader consultation and co-operation. It can also contribute to their personal development. Using the skills of parents as they are needed in particular activities not only enriches the life of the group, but enables parents to show solidarity with their children. For the child's sake, even where the parents show little interest in the church or its message, the leader and the parents should be 'us', not us and them.

Some churches have begun to serve parents in their locality by giving them an opportunity to discuss issues of mutual interest. The extent to which this work can be undertaken depends on local circumstances, say, on what schools and other bodies are doing already. Some churches have received the help of professional people in opening counselling centres for parents and/or adolescents. Others have taken the opportunity to arrange occasional programmes of meetings and have been responsible for inviting a number of specialist consultants. Meetings on topics such as adolescent-parent relationships; drug-taking; Religious Education in day schools; teaching children to pray; some of the problems

associated with large Secondary schools; when and how to
teach children to read; three generations in one household;
play facilities in the area; petty crimes or dishonesty in childhood; and sex education, have been valued by parents. They
have appreciated the initiative of the church. What is meant
by meeting? In some instances, perhaps where there has
been public concern about a problem such as drug-taking or
the provision of play facilities, fifty or a hundred parents, the
majority of whom may have no other church connection,
have gathered in a church hall. In other instances, a handful
of people have met in a private house. In either case, the
most important aspect of the meeting was not the contribution of the consultant, but that ordinary people were given
an opportunity to converse about a matter of importance to
them and to act together on their resolutions. The publication
by the Church of England of its report, *Marriage and the
Church's task*, in 1978, should provoke fresh and informed
discussion of marriage and family matters in local congregations.

Community development
    Community development and community action are two
of the potentially most important developments in Western
society. A. J. Wesson in the paper quoted earlier, says,
'Community developers work with a methodology of discovery; that is, they assume that people and communities
discover their true identity through the experience of living,
and by reflecting upon that experience, not by making that
experience conform to preconceived absolutes.'
    Usually those involved in community action are some of
the less privileged members of society who either on their
own or with a catalyst, have banded together in the face of
an injustice or a threat to the quality of their lives. In *Power
for the powerless: The role of community action*,[27] Robert
Holman writes, 'If the poor are to take collective action,
three further implications follow. Firstly, the opposing
interests of different groups will be made quite explicit.
Secondly, social service organizations will be subjected to
pressure from outside forces. Thirdly, the process by which
change is contemplated will clearly be shown to be political.

It is at these points that community action is regarded as relevant. For community action is a political activity attempting to win power for the powerless.

'The growth of community action, however, has been most notable in two quite different spheres. Local community action groups, composed of the poor and their helpers, have been formed to tackle the immediate needs of neighbourhoods. The best known example concerns the various groups in Notting Hill, but many others can be named – housing action bodies, as in North Islington; tenants' associations, as in Moseley, Birmingham; the work involving so-called "problem" families in Haringey; organizations receive their cohesion from a particular need or condition rather than by neighbourhood. Claimants' Unions, for persons dependent upon social security benefits, have expanded from one branch in 1962 to over twenty-five by 1970. Mothers in Action, a society for unsupported mothers, grew from just over a hundred members in 1968 to over a thousand two years later. Mention, too, should be made of the numerous larger tenants' associations, which hold a place between neighbourhood bodies and national client organizations. The examples are wide and varied, and no consideration can be given to whether squatters and activities stimulated by bodies such as the Young Volunteer Force can be defined as community action. What is clear is that some members of the deprived have decided that the only way to break out of their situation is to align themselves with collective action.'

Both community development and community action enable people to learn by doing. As their corporate effect is taken seriously and as their understanding develops through conversing with colleagues and initiating informed and constructive action the participants grow in self-respect.

In *Building a better community* we read, 'All the churches in Britain have a long history for caring for people in the community. Christians have been in the vanguard of welfare services and now, in a period of economic decline and increasing unemployment, they are needed more than ever in helping people to meet the needs of the community.

'I see the church having responsibilities to the community, sharing in God's mission. I see the mission as not taking God

to the world, but finding out what God is doing in the world
and joining in. The church itself becoming a catalyst in a
neighbourhood.'[28]

Conscientization

Conscientization is the name given to a literacy training
method developed by Paulo Freire in Latin America. As well
as enabling groups to read and write, the method accom-
plishes the more important work of helping the learners to
develop in personal, social and political awareness. Paulo
Freire writes,[29] ' "Conscientization" is a joint project in that
it takes place in a man among other men, men united by
their action and by their reflection upon that action and upon
the world. Thus men together achieve the state of perceptive
clarity which Goldman calls "the maximum of potential
consciousness beyond real consciousness." '

In practice, a leader might gather a group of learners and
in conversation look for a few key words. He might, for
instance, notice that he alone was wearing shoes. The group
would learn the word 'shoe' and begin a discussion about
their shoelessness. Other key words would be noted and the
participants would learn to use them as the discussion pro-
ceeded. As people move from key word to key word they
would be learning not only how to read and write them, they
would be discovering something about their social and political significance. In *Brazil: A profile of poverty*[30] Jenny
Edwards describes a conscientization group.

'. . . A group of families began going to classes. The men
had been laid off work, and the women took up knitting to
earn enough to feed the family. So the theme chosen for the
educational work was "wool". How is wool produced? Who
produces it? What are the systems of land tenure under which
sheep farmers work? Is the system right or wrong? And thence
to the economics and politics of wool production. The group
in question began to understand what they had previously
accepted, and to analyse their own situation. The outcome
was a visit to the local town council. "Would the mayor
please do something about the lack of sanitation facilities?"
The mayor appeared and assured them he would. But they
had learnt. "It is not enough; we would like it in writing,

please. We will wait." And so they sat down and waited until they had a promise of action in writing. And as far as is known, they have their sanitation facilities . . . Only through this kind of social awareness can the *campesino* break out of the vicious circle of poverty under which he has been trapped.'

Addressing the last assembly of the World Council of Christian Education, Col. J. G. Rodriguez, Director Superior of the Ministry of Education in Peru, affirmed that it was through the process of conscientization that Peru would rid itself of under-development and dependence, 'When man possesses a critical attitude towards the reality in which he finds himself, of both the potentialities and limitations of this reality, and of his own limitations to do and be the agent of change for his own benefit and for becoming the new man (humanity)'.

Community action and the process of conscientization are not necessarily Christian. I mention them because they are significant movements which involve ordinary people, often post- or il-literate people, in significant educational and social processes. Western churches which are predominantly middle-class will do well to learn from them, not to discover how to teach people a subject, Christianity, but to find ways to help themselves, other people and society to become Christian.

The meeting place

The majority of churches in the United Kingdom meet in buildings which have already seen years of service. They were built to express the faith and priorities of another age and there was no thought of multi-purpose planning. Flexibility of attitude can be expressed in the style of the church's meeting place and there have been imaginative adaptations of old buildings to make them susceptible to use in a variety of ways.

Anyone building a church now can incorporate flexibility into the design. A large square well illuminated and carpeted area which could be used both for worship and various kinds of group work, perhaps with a number of smaller rooms for groups, would meet the basic requirements. All the furniture would be portable and there would be plenty of space for wall-mounted and free-standing exhibitions. Colour can be added by the use of drapes.

Since it now seems likely that people will spend less and less time in employed work, churches should be able to contribute to the provision of leisure activities and facilities for the meetings of interest groups. The possibility of opening church premises for leisure should make church people think hard about the kind of rooms and standard of comfort they want to make available. In so many churches there is a desperate need for comfortable and well equipped meeting rooms and lounges with audio-visual equipment installed.

A most obvious characteristic of a carefully planned meeting place is that it must be adaptable for many kinds of uses; each kind of activity makes its own demands. The room should probably be adaptable for practical activities, requiring tables with smooth working surfaces and a supply of water not too far distant. Space is needed in which people can talk to each other without everyone overhearing. Ideally for those eleven years old and upwards there should be a number of comfortable chairs and for those younger, a carpeted floor. The celebration of the liturgy may require a more formal arrangement of furniture. Even if the worship were to arise spontaneously and did not require any special furniture, the use of music and the possibility of using drama and other media may be borne in mind.

The basic decoration of the room is best kept simple. Brightly coloured curtains help to make a room attractive. The curtains should be both generous in length and well lined so as to make an effective contribution towards blacking-out the room to make possible the use of projected material. In addition to overhead lighting, one or two free-standing spot-lights are also desirable. These can be used effectively to focus attention on, say, a worship centre or picture or vase of flowers, or to illuminate an exhibition or to create a pool of light. If the floor is carpeted, polythene sheeting can be provided at the appropriate times to protect it from water, paint, sand and plasticine. Display boards, at a height children as well as adults can comfortably use, should be fastened to and painted the same colour as the walls.

Though I have suggested the kind of meeting place which

could most easily be adapted to a wide variety of uses, I do not think that the development of church community activities depends on buildings. Whatever the style of building, where there is a will, which is exercised with imagination, appropriate ways will be found. The mention of will and imagination lead us to think about leadership in a fellowship in which all are learners and all are teachers.

Chapter 7

Preparation for Leadership

Nothing is more important in human terms than the life of a child. Adults must attend to children because it is from them, Jesus implied, they would learn the way into the Kingdom of God. Children must be allowed to teach adults. Conversely no work is more important than helping a child to enjoy beauty and to divine truth; to handle the gentler emotions, to show compassion and to cope with hurt and disappointments; to express feelings and to create imaginatively; to discover priorities; to feel secure in the love that holds all people and to revel in eager zest for living; to develop an inner life, to reflect, and to pray; to realize that in many ways he has power and to explore some of the decisions involved in the exercise of power. But while nothing is more important than this complex ministry shared by adults – parents, teachers, leaders of uniformed organizations and children's and youth clubs, friends and relations – it does not lead me to say, 'Very well, let us concentrate our attention exclusively on the children'. Children cannot be isolated from the real world as part of their preparation for it. They need to overhear adult conversation, to be involved in the decision making of daily life, to confront cynicism and ugliness. The church community contributes most to children when it is conscious of the importance of its ministry to them and is also living realistically in today's world. Throughout this book I have been and am as much concerned with the education of adults as with the education of the young. Preparation for leadership should include all those involved in the leadership of children's and adult groups, but not only those!

Church community: Corporate ministry

A church community approach to education and worship is likely to develop a new form of local team ministry composed of all the leaders of the church. Clergy or ministers,

lay preachers, leaders of children's and of week-day groups
in particular will be involved along with a changing group of
adults. From time to time these may be small group leaders,
resource persons, askers of questions, stimulators of interest
in a theme and contributors of particular skills. The ministry
will become much more that of the whole church; the work
of the clergy or minister will be much more that of the theological consultant, co-ordinator, personnel consultant and
celebrant. In such a team situation, it will not be possible to
draw narrow distinctions between the responsibility of the
worship preparation group and the pastoral care of the
church. A minister describing his experience of a worship
preparation group wrote, 'This group has been my mainstay
as minister, and I could not now imagine how I could ever
have dared to prepare worship without this important preparatory process. In addition the group has been the heart of
my pastoral work. In the group, people have been open with
each other and they have grown as persons. In that atmosphere they have grown to trust each other and the contribution of this fellowship to the church has been of incalculable
value.'

Whole congregation
   The whole congregation of the local church has to be helped
to take its part in the education and nurture of the young.
Love for the young may be expressed in arranging social
occasions when young and old can meet, engaging in social
service or in raising money for a charity together, and the
exchanging of cards at appropriate times of the year. It may
mean embarking on special study action projects which
involve every age group in the church or developing the
church's programme of education and worship into a church
community activity. Above all, care will be expressed through
the interest which shows itself in the willingness of adults to
listen to and talk with children. Children must also be encouraged to lead the adults and to take part in adult conversations.
Many children leave the church without picking up any hint
that Christian faith is fundamentally about living. Perhaps
this is because there has not been enough of the tension,
passion, joy, fear and filth of daily living in their experience

in the community of faith. It is a reflection of the poor quality
of the church community life that many children leave with
only one or two people knowing their names and often no
one knowing their interests, family background and reason
for leaving. To put it at its lowest, the church cannot afford
to be so careless! In speaking of those who work with children
in the church, we are bound to mean in the first instance,
everyone who is part of the church. All must bear responsibility. First we shall think about the education of clergy and
ministers and then about the preparation of leaders and
helpers for the kind of approach and work I have outlined.

Ministerial education

It seems reasonable to ask, in view of the potential development of a church community approach and since the first
prerequisite of ministerial training – a good general education
– can be obtained in State institutions, whether separated
training in ministerial training colleges is the most suitable
approach. Already words have betrayed us! Ministerial training, the phrase normally used of preparation for the full-time
service of the church, presupposes (through the use of the
word 'training') that those who are responsible for such
courses know what the candidate needs to be trained in; they
know what he must know and they can equip him with such
skills as will qualify him – trained! The term 'education for
the ministry of the church' leaves the end result of the learning process much more open and carries the implication that
ministry belongs to the church rather than to one man or
woman.

Experiential courses

To return to our question: Do we need separated education
for the ministry in church colleges? As long as a good general
education can be prescribed as an entrance qualification,
ministerial education could become part of an advanced adult
Christian Education course of a kind which, though it might
not be undertaken by the local church, could be organized in
a number of the larger centres of population. There seems to
be no difference between what a minister needs to enable
him to do his work and what an intelligent lay person needs

to enable him to be a responsible member of society and a contributor to the ministry of the church. There is much to be said for the stimulation and encouragement of learning together. Such a course could be an evening or 'spare time' activity following the good precedent of the Open University or various diocesan ordination training schemes. Qualification for ordination would depend on a candidate gaining a certain number of credits by having satisfactorily completed the appropriate number of courses. The experience of Open University students underlines the importance of short periods spent apart for intensive work in University halls of residence or well equipped conference centres.

In making this suggestion I am not forgetting the University faculties of theology which of course would continue to serve those wishing to make an academic study of a particular theological, biblical or historical discipline. I am simply drawing a distinction between such study which need not presuppose Christian commitment, and education for ministry. Education for the ministry would be much more concerned with the handling of experience than with learning a subject. The student would not be expected to study a course in theology and then by chance discover such insights as there may be in it to help him to understand and handle a practical problem. Rather, he would begin with the practical problem and treat it as a theological entity. The following may help to explain the phrase 'theological entity'. In their first week in a college of education a group of students (all Christians) who were specializing in Religious Education and three-quarters of whom had passed 'A' level Religious Knowledge were taken into a neighbouring school at playtime. Then they were asked to say how they had understood what they had seen in terms of Religious Education. There was silence. Their training/education had been in a subject rather than a life and it was some time before they could grasp that the sharing, playing, laughter, fighting, loving, hating and friendship they had witnessed were the very stuff of Christian thought. At a later stage they might be expected to see the institution itself as raising theological questions. Theology they had to learn, was a way of seeing, hearing and thinking about life with the clues of Jesus and Christian experience, rather than simply handling a body of knowledge.

The student will be stimulated to read theology as he is involved in the processes of thinking in a Christian way, and in learning to use Christian clues and the evidence of Christian experience.[31] That this is almost always an inter-disciplinary task could be recognized in the tutors appointed and would further be made evident in the insights which others on the course may be able to contribute. The student would grapple with the central activities of the work of the ministry – leadership of groups, pastoral work and personnel management, understanding institutions, the church's relationship to statutory bodies, and the leadership of worship – by reflecting on actual experience. Each course would be based on a life issue and a generous allowance of time would have to be made for reading and for writing up and reflecting on experience. In each case the student would be expected to show that he had understood the contribution of the disciplines most connected with the life issue concerned, had attempted to think theologically about it, had used the Bible, and perhaps brought historical and international perspectives to bear on the issue. The major courses (life issues) might be found within: a social problem; creating worship; how people learn; leadership and management; handling an international issue; local and national politics; pastoral counselling; the meaning of mission; communications and media.

Radical re-think

It seems much more creative at this time of loss of confidence in traditional ministerial training and of financial stress in church life to think of new approaches than to look for ways of re-vamping the old. Even those colleges which at present include an education course in their curriculum do not, or because of academic links cannot, allow the educational implications of the course to influence other parts of the curriculum. Now is the appropriate time for radical re-thinking to take account of educational insights and a wider understanding of ministry.

Whether such a radical re-thinking of education for ministry actually takes place remains to be seen. There is no doubt that the development of the community of the church and the approaches to learning and teaching I have outlined, will involve clergymen and ministers, as much as lay people, in a new preparation for leadership, if according to my understanding of it, they are to be the Church for this age.

Leaders and helpers

Throughout I have referred to those who are specifically appointed to work with children in the church as 'leaders', 'workers', or 'helpers'. No language is absolutely satisfactory but, in view of our understanding of the church community and of education, it seems better to speak of 'church', 'leaders of children's groups', and 'helpers', and of age 'groups', than to use any other terminology. The popular connotation of the word 'teacher', though it does as great an injustice to much day school education as to any other, does not suggest the corporate nature of the learning experience we have emphasized; and for some, its associations are too authoritarian to have any place in church education. Carl Rogers makes some interesting observations about teaching in *On becoming a person*.[7] '1. My experience has been that I cannot teach another person how to teach. 2. It seems to me that anything that can be taught to another is relatively inconsequential, and has little or no significant influence on behaviour. 3. I realise increasingly that I am only interested in learnings which significantly influence behaviour. 4. I have come to feel that the only learning which significantly influences behaviour is self-discovered, self-appropriated learning. 5. Such self-discovered learning, truth that has been personally appropriate and assimilated in experience, cannot be directly communicated to another. 6. As a consequence of the above, I realise that I have lost interest in being a teacher.' This view may in part be countered by those who are able to point to a 'teacher' who was a decisive influence for good in their lives.

In 1972 the Methodist Church began a brave programme of education through which it was hoped that all those working with children in Methodist churches would receive a basic training. In some ways this reflected moves made by the uniformed organizations to exclude leaders who had not first been trained by them. Other churches run training courses, and there has been for a number of years an Inter-Church

Training Group which has promoted short ecumenical training courses in a number of centres in the United Kingdom. It is desirable that everyone charged with the responsibility of working with children in the church should have been helped to think about the development of children, how children learn, practical learning activities, how children worship, the Bible and its use with children, children and the church community, the preparation of the meeting place, the use of equipment, and story-telling.

The example of the leader is important. The leader should communicate that he or she is a learner, eager, alongside the children, to go on learning. Those local churches which cannot appoint adults who will take their responsibility seriously should face the possibility of not undertaking specific work among children. This could mean that parents would be faced with responsibility for the Christian education of their children. It may be argued that in any case more parents should do more in this respect, but the small family unit is not a varied or stimulating enough community to stand as a substitute for a church community. Inability to find adult leaders could result in the developing of church life so that the whole church community assumed responsibility.

'. . . Church X was in the midst of looking for new staff for two departments when an elder asked, "Why do we need departments?" The question began a series of serious discussion which led to the creation of a new Christian education programme. It was decided that 3–4 and 5–6 year old children needed a traditional group or department structure; the continuity of relationship week by week with established members of staff was important. But no member of staff should serve longer than two years without a break of several months. It was agreed that the older children did not need a rigid department structure and that it was important that children of eight years upwards should be enabled to discover the Christian community as a whole, rather than know only one or two "teachers".

'A Christian education committee was elected. The secretary was also appointed as co-ordinator. A second member was in charge of visual aids and equipment. A third was responsible for adult education, linking with the adult organizations, organizing house groups and confirmation or church membership courses. A fourth member was personnel manager; his task was to discover some of the talents and gifts, experiences and insights of adult members of the congregation so that when people were needed to lead groups the most appropriate person could be approached. The fifth member of the committee was the group planner. Working with the minister he planned the number of groups necessary for a particular theme. All group leaders, whether they were former leaders and helpers in the children's departments or not, attend a preparation class.

'Through this scheme, many more people have got to know the children. It has been possible to use both peer groups and family groups in which young people of different ages learn together. The members of each group wear a coloured badge throughout each course as a means of easy recognition. The planning of groups and the appointing of leaders is completed two months in advance.'

Essential preparation

G. H. Archibald began the practice, still maintained in some churches, of insisting that only those leaders and helpers who had attended the appropriate preparatory meeting were allowed to work with children on the subsequent Sunday or Sundays. If that principle was justifiable in the 'twenties and 'thirties, it is likely to be more justifiable now when methods and activities are much more complicated. In spite of all the difficulties churches have in finding leaders and helpers, this kind of rule shows the seriousness of the church towards its work among children – or more properly, towards its ministry of education for children and adults – and is to be commended. The pastoral problems caused by such a rule are worth facing in view of the improvements such a standard of commitment can contribute to the church's ministry of education.

Church statistics are a far from adequate guide to church life, but they support the impression gained in conversations in many parts of the country that inadequately prepared leaders – and poor church communities – not only lose children from the church, they lose adults too.

Whichever leader preparation courses are used, the importance of certain aspects of the preparation, which sometimes have scant treatment, should be stressed.

Adult thought

It is important that leaders and helpers should first think through the topic they are handling at an adult level before they try to answer the question: What shall we do with the children? Many leaders either rush into practical considerations too quickly or think only at the level of the children with whom they are working; in either case because they have never explored it for themselves they tend to trivialize the theme for the children. For instance, the leader who is content to handle the Christmas story at the level of its being a pretty story about shepherds, a star, wise men and a baby in a manger, is unlikely to be able to communicate the wonder and mystery of incarnation. The leader who has never faced the fact that he erects barriers between himself and others is unlikely to be able to help young people, through an exploration of Christian love, to enter into mature open relationships. This emphasis on thinking first at an adult level raises further questions about who is the leader or helper.

G. H. Archibald used to insist that young people should be given an opportunity to express their Christian commitment in service. He argued that working with children provided an ideal opportunity. Young people were 'ploughed back' as helpers with the 5–6 year olds. 'There is a time during mid-adolescence when social emotions rise into consciousness and must be called into full life through activity, or they will atrophy. One outlet for this urge to be doing, is to teach a class of little children of size and age not impossible to manage. Take your young people and under the best leader you can find, put them to work. While leading them to the understanding of children, help them to comprehend their own developing nature and God's purposes for humankind . . . The young people come into it at the right moment in their lives, just when they are spoiling for something to do . . . The leaders soon proved that these classes must be a real training ground . . . where knowledge of the

Bible was pursued, and matters pertaining to the spiritual life were seriously considered.'[32] It is unfortunate that Archibald's principle that young people need opportunities to engage in worthwhile work alongside adults has to a large extent been lost and there has developed the degenerate practice of allowing young teenagers to act as leaders. If, as I wish to insist, the church is a learning, teaching, serving, witnessing and worshipping community in which all are learners and all are teachers, there will be a place for adolescents, as for older people, as helpers in the children's groups. But they must not be the responsible leaders. Children should not be entrusted to people who are at an age at which parents would never contemplate entrusting their children in day schools.

Ordinary experience -- ecumenical education

Since it is now generally accepted that Christian education should begin in experience and lead to experience, leaders will continually have to handle issues that come from ordinary human experience. This requires a thoughtful, sensitive (inter-disciplinary) approach. In practice a leader has to be ready to theologize off-the-cuff about life issues as conversation and activity offer him appropriate opportunities and to express himself in language suited to the age and experience of the children or adults with whom he is working. This is a theological exercise of greater subtlety than most theological college students are expected to undertake.

The task is made the more difficult because there is no one Christian view about many life issues. Take any of the major news items of the day and Christians will be found holding differing, even opposing, views. The same is true of the most ordinary domestic and personal matters. In consequence, as well as knowing what counts in the forming of Christian attitudes to public life and private experience, leaders must also be able to cope with differences of opinion and understanding. The frank recognition of such differences does not lessen our responsibility to look and to work for their reconciliation.

Helping leaders to think in a Christian way about life issues is, therefore, of paramount importance in their preparation.

For instance, leaders should be helped to answer such questions as: What is specifically Christian about many of the life issues within the experience of a six year old – home, friends, helping, discovering? An answer cannot be found in a few biblical texts; it depends on a doctrine of man and belief about the nature of God. A leader who has explored for himself aspects of the complex interplay of theological reflection, biblical insight, historic and contemporary experience and thought will have something to say to a child who is quick enough to ask the penetrating question: 'Well, what is Christian about being friends, lots of people are friends who are not Christians?' He will be able to help the child to explore possible answers to the question. A child who finds an answer for himself not only begins to create his own theology, but also learns skills which will help him to find and handle evidence and to answer other questions. To be enabled to search for an answer and to be aware of the constructive critical process by which it was reached is education; to be told an answer is at best training, at worst indoctrination.

This matter of handling issues which grow out of ordinary human experience is part of what Dr. Ulrich Becker calls 'ecumenical education'. In World Council of Churches papers[33] he has drawn attention to the traditional meaning of that term: Education which helps people to understand the faith and practices of other Christians and to make a serious and responsible commitment to the ecumenical movement. Dr. Becker has also helped us to understand 'ecumenical' as referring to the churches' life in the world. He asks, 'How is the "training for world citizenship", or "the formation of the responsible consciousness regarding the one world to come", or "the preparation of people for commitment in the struggle for justice" related to the ecumenical vision of God's will for one fully committed fellowship in all places and in all ages?'

The ecumenical context of the educational work of the local church must be stressed and explored by those whose task is to help to create the new *oikoumene*.

How people learn

Time must be found in leadership preparation to explore

how people learn. Fundamental as this is to the work of the Church, few churches have taken it into account in church life generally. The learning processes of both children and adults are the same in church as in any other mixed community. Though many of the techniques we use are used also in schools, the best model for the learning community of the church is the family. A number of simple activities can be used to stimulate discussion in one or more sessions. A short introductory course which has been used with many groups of leaders is included in the Appendix A.

Music and singing

The place of music in the learning programme should be explored. At a time when music plays so important a part in the lives of many young people and adults, it is surprising that mood music and musical signals are used so little in church life. But it is a matter for considerable satisfaction that so much attention in recent years has been given to the writing of songs and hymns which reflect contemporary life.

Music and singing facilitate non-cognitive experiences which along with painting, spontaneous drama, some forms of community service and friendship in the church community, are valuable counter-balances to programmes heavily dominated by cognitive learning. The emotional quality in music and singing can be a most appropriate vehicle for expressing both the deeper and gentler emotions, and the profound aspirations, responses and themes of Christian faith. People are often involved more spontaneously in music and singing than in many other activities. A few children and adults are unable to enjoy any musical experience but their number does not constitute a major problem. The major problem associated with the use of music is that of manipulation or indoctrination.

There is an element of manipulation in every human activity. Every medium contains its own, sometimes hidden, messages. The church has always to be vigilant to spot its own unspoken assumptions and expectations and to maintain a rigorous open-endedness. The churches do not want church members who have not first experienced the liberation of being equipped to make responsible choices for themselves.

The possibility of a person choosing against Christianity must always be real in a programme that claims the description 'education'.

The problem is that emotional and credal conviction expressed in music is sometimes too strong. The most creative way to handle this is to use hymns to summarize experience, to focus shared concern or to restate previously expressed conviction.

It is of immense value to appoint a resource person (where a suitable person can be found) to whom leaders can turn for help in choosing music, particularly recorded music, which can be used in the exploration of a theme in worship.

Use of quietness

If modern educational practice is taken seriously, there will be a stress on activity (learning by doing) and on learning from each other. These are lessons leaders of adult groups particularly need to learn: what we do we remember, what we use we know. Conversely there remains the need also to help leaders, children and adults to use silence.

Most people live with a background hum of electric machines, the rumble of traffic, the distant noise of aircraft and the noises and voices of other people. Many live with a background of broadcast music. Church buildings are far from silent. Rather than talking of silence, it is probably more accurate to use the somewhat relative term of quietness. To be able to sit still and quiet, not because of tiredness, is important in the process of personal reflection and prayer. Children and adults should be helped to use quietness, to gaze at flowers or a beautiful object or to repeat slowly and silently precious words from the Bible, a poem or a prayer. This might begin with only a short period of quietness but since the practice of stillness needs as much practising as any other skill, it should be done often and the length of time spent in quietness increased gradually. In a remarkable paper, the Rev. H. A. Hamilton wrote:

'Alongside my continuing sense of vocation to the Christian ministry there persists an oft-repeated longing for the growth of an inner awareness of the reality of the Spirit and for the power to live in that dimension of life. For me that longing was born in my first year at college when I joined a group resolved to begin the day with a "Morning Watch". It was renewed on the occasion of my reception into the Congregational Union with other young ministers in 1924 when Dr. Robert Horton said to us, "I am not going to ask you men whether you know how to preach: I am going to ask you, 'Do you know how to pray and can you teach others to pray?'" That question has haunted me all through my ministry, it returned to me when I became Young People's Secretary to the denomination and came pointedly again when I had students to train at Westhill College. It seemed the crucial test when I returned to the pastoral ministry and it remains my longing still.

'I have had enough times of illumination to desire more; enough times of companionship with an unseen presence to long for it all the time. Today, that is sharpened by the current quest for awareness of the Transcendental, and deepened by pleas like Kathleen Gibberd's in the *Guardian* of January 10th 1973, when she asked why there was no attempt in schools to train children in the Mystic Way.

'Reading in current literature confirms this. There is F. G. Happold in his Pelican Book on *Mysticism*, half discussion and half anthology, who quotes an instruction from Boehme to the disciple: "Cease from thine own activity, fix thine eye upon one point . . . Gather all thoughts and by faith press into the centre . . . Be silent before the Lord, sitting alone with Him in thy inmost and secret all . . ." Or T. S. Eliot's unforgettable words: "And prayer is more than an order of words, or the sound of a voice praying. And what the dead had no words for when living they can tell you being dead. The communication of the dead is tongued with fire beyond the language of the living." These are words which open new horizons to the world of the spirit; they reveal new depths of the divine.

'How can we find a pattern of mind and a habit of life which pave the way to the place where we can be more fully aware of the presence of the Spirit and of the living Word within the words, and how can it be taught to others?

'There is a mighty affirmation by Martin Buber which serves as a lively starting point for such a venture. He says: "We are

being addressed." The belief that the Spirit of God is addressing mankind in the continuous creation, that he confronts
them in ventures and the needs of their fellows, and speaks
positively to any man who is willing and eager to listen, this
is the foundation principle through which earthly man can
possess a life of the Spirit.

'How shall we proceed? There is one golden rule; it is
attention. In her *Waiting on God*, Simone Weil pursues this
discipline as the sovereign way to awareness. She says that
the underlying purpose of all education is to teach or to
practice attention. Whether Maths or Language or Science,
they train our capacity to attend. This is the faculty we most
need if we are to hear how we are being addressed and if we
are to be able to respond.

'We may begin anywhere, with any object or scene which
initially holds our attention or "addresses us". We respond,
focusing all our energy of vision and mind upon it until we
cease to be conscious of ourselves looking and pass into the
very being of what we are beholding. We continue to hold
ourselves to the object and to hold it to us, until something is
"given". What we see wholly, begins to speak "of itself", a
new language of its own, a divine visual language. We say
"wholly" because into our looking must go all our ways of
knowing: any observations or scientific knowing, any external
appreciations or aesthetic enjoyment, all such knowing must
be included and transcended in this act of single, responsive
looking.

'When we can hold or be held no longer and return "home-
ward to habitual self", we shall return with an enrichment of
life. If we extend our range of "exposure" so that we attend
and are open, a variety of scenes, all of which speak beyond
the appearances of things; if we go on to be able to relate one
such experience to another, we are likely to find that every-
thing belongs together, to one order of being and that the
same timeless words are being repeated.

'Once practice has confirmed this way of looking, we may
extend the character as well as the range of our vision. "God"
is the Lord of all created life and addresses us everywhere,
but especially he uses the personal dealings of men with each
other as his language. Biography and history tell of him, to

those who know how to listen; the individual encounters of
daily life and the human events which make up our contemporary world are ways in which he draws near to us, but only
when we are on the look-out do we hear him. When we are
in the midst of people and involved in what is happening it is
not easy to do this. But when we are able to retire from
immediate encounter and recollect in tranquillity awhile, then
we can see people and behaviour at a new depth and if we go
on holding people in our imagination, we can hear what the
Spirit is saying and, maybe, what he is wanting us to do.
Moreover, if we persist in this practice of withdrawal and of
humble looking, we may well grow in the capacity to see
aright and to hear at the very moment of encounter.

'Such practice fulfils our intentions in the act of Interces-
sion. To be able to hold the image of those for whom we
would pray and carry them forward with us into the presence
of God and crave for them the power of Christ is a costly
effort; a real going forth of the self; but it makes prayer real.
And if this extends to our direct relation to Jesus Christ so
that "we see him who is invisible" then indeed we have
glimpses of Heaven. To help us are creative works, sculptures
and pictures which represent him in action and in contempla-
tion. These are not so much attempted likenesses of him as
images which project the Spirit of him in whose face man
beheld the glory of God. There can be a picture for a mood
or an attitude and we can learn to look through these, in fact
"to look at him until we find him looking back at us".

'These are all simple ways to practice the presence of God.
They are open not to disputation but to experiment. These
are a beginning of the ways in which I have learned that all
existence is alive with him and that, indeed and indeed, he
is addressing us. They are also ways simple to teach. The
encouragement of these practical steps may well bring a reality to "learning to pray" which is much more the development of an attitude than a knowledge of the words. If words
there be, what are better than these:

"Look graciously on us, O Lord, and grant us
for our hallowing, thoughts that pass into
prayer, prayer that passes into love, and
love that passes into life with Thee for ever." '[34]

Learning to create worship

Quietness is only one aspect of worship; the traditional elements of worship – adoration, confession, supplication, thanksgiving and so on – all presuppose the ability of the worshipper to reflect on his own experience of life and on the Gospel. Acts of worship also presuppose an ability on the part of the participants to worship. Young people can be seen in what might be called a secular attitude of worship as they scream in adulation of a popular singer or hero worship a star football player. Those who lead worship might learn from such observation that young people usually only get to the point of worship as a result of considerable audio-visual and, often times, group stimulation. Perhaps this is why worship at residential conferences seems to have a special significance. One of the urgent functions of the preparation group is to give leaders the opportunity to reflect on their own experience and to incite each other to worship. What they cannot do with adult support they are unlikely to be able to lead children to do.

In practice, this could mean that as the preparation group thinks at an adult level about the theme of a course one or two members of the group could be responsible for seeing how elements in the conversation could be used to lead into worship. Their contribution to the conversations would be to incite worship – at an appropriate point during the meeting or at its conclusion – and to lead it. In this way, they could be engaged in an activity which is similar to that required of them in leading children's or adult groups where worship cannot be formally structured or planned in detail beforehand. Though some elements of worship would have been selected before the session, the actual act of worship must grow out of the shared experience and learning activity. After leading other adults in worship, the leader can benefit from hearing the constructive comments of his peers who may have seen for instance, how the shared experience could have been used differently, how music could have been added, how much help and co-operation could have been sought from the participants, where a picture might have helped, where an opportunity to express commitment might have been appropriate for some participants, how a particular passage of the Bible might have spoken into the common experience . . . Leaders should be open and trusting enough with each other to be able to make and to receive constructive critical comments. The critical comments of children may not be spoken (though they should be encouraged to speak them), but they will be no less real because of that. They may be more significant: children vote with their feet.

Aims and expectations

Research has shown that the expectations a teacher entertains of the children he teaches profoundly affects his teaching and their performance. In August 1967 the *New York Times* featured on its front page an account of research undertaken by Dr. Robert Rosenthal under the heading, 'Study indicates pupils do well when teacher is told they will.' It described tests in which rats performed far better after the experimenters had been told, falsely, that the rats had been specially bred for intelligence. The same kind of rats turned into poor performers when the experimenters had been told the animals were dull. Professor Rosenthal then began similar tests on school-children, with what he termed similar results. A random sample of first- and second-grade children at a South San Francisco elementary school, who it was predicted would make dramatic gains in schoolwork, actually made those gains, while the rest of the student body did not. Only the teachers and not the pupils or parents had been told of the predictions. Postman and Weingartner comment on this report:

'We can assume that the rats were behaving neither "intelligently" nor "stupidly". They were just behaving. Whether such behaviour is intelligent or stupid has less to do with their behaviour than it does with a human perception and evaluation of that behaviour. What happened was this: the experimenters, having classified the rats as "intelligent", selected those bits of behaviour, those wiggles, that would be consistent with the label. They saw intelligent behaviour because that is what they expected to see. Experimenters looking at rats they believed to be dull saw "dull" behaviour for the same reason. What we see is a product of what we believe to be "out there". We see things not as *they* are, but as *we* are.

'The case of the elementary school children is quite similar, but with an additional dimension. The teachers perceived these children as intelligent because they were expecting to see "intelligent" behaviour. The teachers, like the laboratory experimenters, *made* the reality that was there. But we can assume that once the teachers made that reality, the children began to make one of their own. The children modified their behaviour in accordance with the positive expectations of their teachers. In other words, the children changed their perceptions of themselves, and they did so because their environment had a positive effect on their purposes and assumption.'[12]

If this is true in respect of day school teachers, it is likely also to be true of church workers. I have sometimes seen a lack of expectation communicated through a leader's hesitation as he introduced, say, the idea of improvised drama into a group. That the children will not respond is often due to the language and attitude of the leader who communicates his expectation that they would not like to respond.

There are implications here for both the leader as an individual and for the preparation group. Taking the latter first, the overall aim of the educational programme of the church should be discussed frequently. Since the aim is so potentially enormous – to do with personal fulfilment, social awareness, appreciation of the gentler emotions and of beauty, a sense of historic continuity in the community of faith, awareness of Jesus, growth in faith, commitment, learning to worship, a critique of society, the use of time and talents and so on and on, and above all to do with God, it is more than likely that particular local churches will have their distinctive emphases. Within the overall framework there will be agreed short-term emphases. The aims should be discussed by all the leaders in the church so that there is a church policy about education. The church should know the direction in which its work is pointing and should be able critically to assess its effectiveness.[35] Suppose a church believes that when a person is confirmed or becomes a church member he is in effect saying about himself something like, 'I respond to Jesus Christ who claims me and I want to work out the meaning of this for myself and society in a committed fellowship'. That church may need a different style of church life and educational programme from one which believes that at the same point a person is saying, 'I have been saved by the shedding of Christ's blood and give myself to him'.

Having established a church education policy it should be possible for leaders to believe that the children, young people and adults with whom they are working have the potential in them to fulfil the aim of the programme. I mean this, not in the sense that the leaders believe that the church has to leap an academic hurdle, nor that they can manage without the gift of the Spirit or a sense of the call and fascination of Jesus. Rather, the leader must believe the best of every person with whom he works and listen attentively to what each child or adult says. He must not work out his expectations in his own terms only, but allow the children and adults to contribute their expectations. If he does, the children and adults will continually contribute to the reviewing of the church's educational aims: after all, all are teachers and all are learners. This will happen only if the leader has high expectations and shows his trust and confidence in the people with whom he works.

Preparing together

Only where it is quite unavoidable, say in some country districts, should leaders and helpers prepare or work on their own. Two things are involved. First, leaders should stimulate each other in preparation and receive stimulation from ministers and other adults. But more than stimulation is at stake. The complexity of human life means that we need the help we can give to each other to understand our world, the children or adults in our group, and the meaning of the gospel for our times. Leaders need each other. Perhaps one of the reasons for the failure of some training classes is that leaders need a richer meeting than can be provided by many local churches. In spite of the effort, travel and time involved, an ecumenical meeting involving leaders from a number of local churches might provide a much needed forum and preparation unit. Second, leaders need help in learning how to use newer techniques and methods. Further, to submit, as part of this process, to the constructive criticisms of one's colleagues can be a most helpful discipline. Few leaders of church groups will be able to observe themselves on video tape in the way that is now common for students in colleges of education, though sometimes this can be arranged through the good offices of teachers in schools or colleges. As an alternative, a leader may lead a group in front of other leaders with a view to hearing their comments later. This method has been used in Australia with good effect.

One of the most interesting comments about preparation groups is that those who lead them ignore the educational principles they expect leaders to use in children's and adult groups: often they are leader dominated. The emphasis in a preparation group should be on leaders, helpers and others learning together in an educational experience as rich and varied as any programme they might hope to lead. That is to say, it has to be conceived as an event in its own right, not simply as a meeting called to prepare a particular session. Rather than talking about techniques or a theme, the participants should be involved in their use or exploration.

Postscript

I have tried in this short book to share my insights into Christian education in the church; it has meant taking a closer look at the nature of the community of faith. My interest in Christian education began when I was a chaplain in a geriatric hospital. There I heard the sometimes horrifying accounts elderly people gave of their childhood experiences in church – and at home. From that beginning the rest you know or can discover from a year book. Now my major concern is with the future – of people and of society. It is to make our contribution to the creation of a new future – of the new man and the new earth – that I believe God is now calling Christian educators. That is why, rightly or wrongly, I have shared my insights. Whatever path of Christian education we tread the responsibility is great, the task is urgent, the goal and its blessing always greater. To work!

APPENDICES

Appendix A

AN INTRODUCTORY COURSE ON HOW PEOPLE LEARN

How do people learn?

Most people will readily respond to the question, 'How do young children learn at home?'

Compile a list of answers and where it will be helpful, discuss them.

Read part of the poem, *Contact*, by Ceciley Taylor.

> What I say to you
> may not be
> what you hear
>
> What I see
> will look different
> through your window:
>
> What I hear
> may be upon a frequency
> untuned by you: . . .[36]

What do we see?

What do we see? Show the following diagrams and note that people see different things. Some see straight lines, others curved lines (figures 1 and 2); some see lines of the same length, others do not (figures 3 and 4); some can find the cube in figure 5, others cannot. The alternating figures in figure 6 are clear to some and some sense movement in figure 7 while others do not. Is the superimposed shape in figure 8 a square or not?

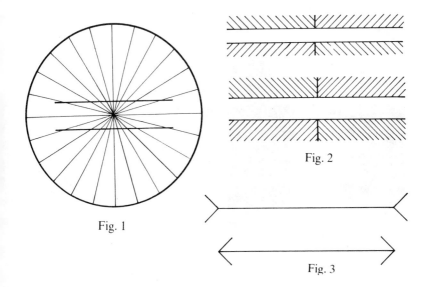

Fig. 1

Fig. 2

Fig. 3

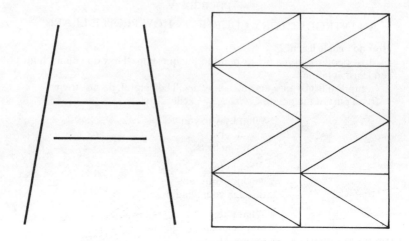

Fig. 4   Fig. 5

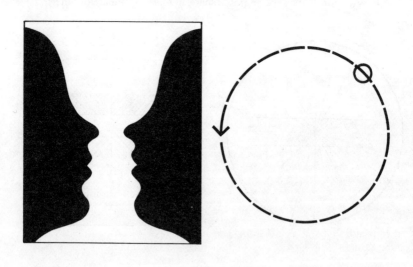

Fig. 6   Fig. 7

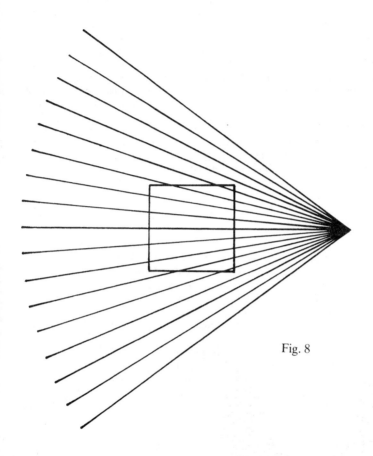

Fig. 8

After this I have shown the leaders a picture or set of pictures and asked them to make a one word response in answer to the question: What is this picture about? Often the pictures used have been published by Christian Aid or Oxfam. A picture of a group of children in a field with their goats, with a couple of shacks in the background, has elicited responses as varied as care, possessions, apprehension, lush growth, games, fun. Or a picture of four children setting off from their not very good looking home, with their mother smiling on the step in the background, has elicited the responses, church, school, best clothes, poor housing, priorities, affection. This brief exercise has been followed by discussion: To what extent do our interests, or understanding of the 'third world', condition what we see?

What do we hear?

What do we hear? Read the following paragraph. After they have heard it, ask the leaders to write down what they think was the main point in the paragraph. When this has been done, ask them to share their answers to the question. It is likely that there will be such variations as: it was about a brave woman; she identified herself with others; she was committed to prison for no good reason; she was determined enough to write in secret; the paragraph advertises a book; women in South Africa are deprived. A group of twenty people can produce as many as nine different main points.

'Helen Joseph is a prisoner in her own house in South Africa. She has been a teacher and social worker but because she worked with the deprived coloured and African women, especially in their opposition to the Government's practice of banishing innocent people without trial to live sometimes hundreds of miles away from their homes, she was arrested and condemned. House arrest means she has no opportunity to work or to meet friends. Mrs. Joseph, an Englishwoman from Sussex, has chosen to stay in South Africa because she believes in equal rights for people of every race and colour. A book which she wrote was sent out by post a few pages at a time and compiled by a friend in England. It is worth reading and may be available from your local library.'[37]

Discussion of this exercise is likely to raise questions about the value of verbal teaching. Further, questions may be asked about the function of a sermon. Does the sermon inform, or educate, or is it most valuable as an inspirational experience in which the verbal detail is of no lasting consequence?

Does the combination of words and images make our communication easier? In the following game ask everyone not to let others see what they write or draw. Give a person a word and ask him to draw what the word represents. Then give another person the drawing, but not the word, and ask him to put a word to it. Then pass on the word without the drawing. Five or six people can be involved. At the end see if particular words or images have meant significantly different things to different people. Useful starter words are: prayer, hand, love, home, peace, flower. Alternatively the exercise may begin with an image. The following (figures 9 and 10) illustrate the progress of the exercise beginning with image:

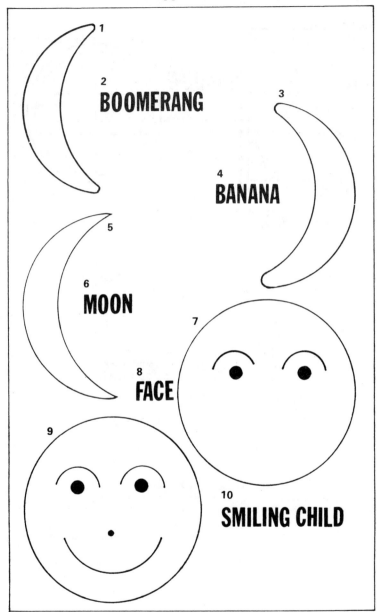

Fig. 9

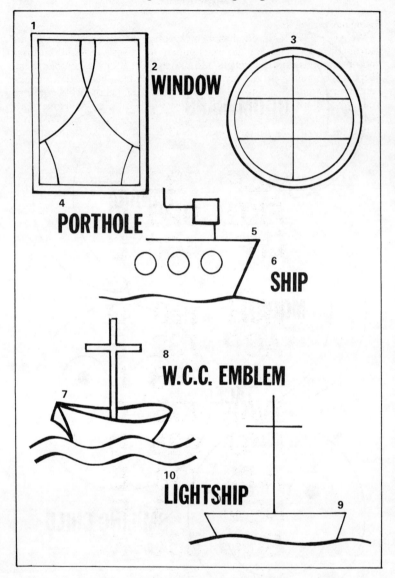

Fig. 10

Though this exercise is open to the criticism that it is contrived, or only a game, useful discussion can be provoked.

Using our memories

We take it for granted that memory plays an important part in the learning process. But how do we stimulate the memory? Read out three motor car registration numbers and ask the leaders to remember them. Repeat the numbers or display them. Continue with other work for five or ten minutes and then return to the numbers. Few people will be able to remember more than one number. Most will be able to remember only part of a number and some will claim to remember nothing. Display a longer list of numbers which includes the three that were to be remembered; the leaders will probably be able to pick them out.

ACP 732 F
FKU 925 D
LYF 480 L

Fig. 11

HJH 190 D
ACP 732 F
NGP 768 L
WAK 105 C
FKU 925 D
AJX 158 E
NEM 5 E
SOO 530 K
BSC 348
LYF 480 L

Fig. 12

Discussion of this exercise could begin with the question: How can you help the people in your group to remember? Sometimes leaders begin a session by asking if those present remember what was done in the previous week. This is almost bound to have a deadening effect, whereas if there were a number of audio and visual clues most people would both remember and be stimulated. Another discussion growing out of this exercise, could be about what people should be asked to remember. The leaders could list some of the things they were asked to remember as children – dates, theorems, names of battles – the details of which have been forgotten. Have these been forgotten because they were not learned as tools to use? How much detail of the Jewish-Christian story do Christians need to remember? And what would it mean to learn such detail as a tool to use?

Does the order in which we learn things matter? Ask the group to say the line preceding, 'Give us this day our daily bread'. Most will be able to do so only by starting at the beginning of the Lord's Prayer.

The order in which things are learned dominates our remembering. For instance, though the third verse of most hymns has been sung frequently as the first, it is the first verse and particularly the first line which is remembered. This, incidentally, draws attention to the importance of careful selection of hymns and songs for children. They will carry into old age an assortment of first lines. I have heard patients in a geriatric hospital reciting to themselves the first lines of children's hymns which could be of little spiritual benefit to them.

Importance of experience

How can we share with others what we believe is important? If the group is a large one divide it into small groups and ask a representative from each group to come outside the room to the leader of the session. Show the representatives something they are unlikely to have seen before, say a persimmon fruit, and then ask them to go back to their groups and to share their experience verbally. Allow only a minute or so before asking for another representative from each group to come out. This time let them handle the fruit so that they experience its weight and the texture of its skin as well as see its shape and colour. Give them paper and crayons and ask them to share their experience audio-visually. After a few minutes ask for a third representative. Give them a fruit each and ask them to let each member of their group handle it before it is cut open, divided into pieces and eaten by the group.

When the fruit has been handled and eaten the members of the group have a common experience of the persimmonness of persimmon. At that point it is worthwhile knowing the name 'persimmon'. They can relate their experience to others' and use others' experience. Though it would have been possible by knowing the name earlier, to have used books to learn about persimmon – to discover, say, how it grows, where it grows, or various ways in which it can be eaten – it would have been an academic exercise. Now the use of books (the experience of others) builds upon the experience of the members of the group.

In discussion ask if the exercise says anything to the members of the group about the importance of experience in the learning process. Can a parallel be drawn between communicating this subtle thing, the persimmonness of persimmon, and sharing difficult Christian concepts? Does the exercise suggest that it is more appropriate to use the experience of the Bible, Church history and the world church at one point in the learning process than another? I have often used the following quotation from Earl Kelley at the conclusion of discussion on this exercise, 'Now it comes about that what we tell the learner, he will make something that is all his own of it, and it will be different from what we held so dear and attempted to "transmit". He will build it into his own scheme of things and relate it uniquely to what he already uniquely holds as experience. Thus he will build a world all his own, and what is really important is what he makes of what we tell him, not what we intended.'[25] Or Helen Coppen's words, 'Meaning is largely gained by the active comparison of a particular response with past experiences'.[38]

On one occasion when I led this exercise a woman demonstrated the power of experience vividly and, thereby, the difficulty we may all have of changing our minds. On hearing the description of the fruit given by the first representative she decided he was speaking about a tomato. The description and drawing of the second representative confirmed her in this opinion even though there were certain things about the drawing that made it look unlike a tomato. When she was confronted with the persimmon she dealt with an evident internal conflict by refusing to taste the fruit but maintained that it was 'only a tomato'. Experience determines our perception! The question then to be faced by the group was, how could we help the woman to change her mind? It was decided, not surprisingly, that the way forward was to frustrate her in the use of her experience. It was arranged that she should use persimmon in a manner in which she commonly used tomato. So slices of persimmon were placed on the top of a cauliflower cheese and placed under a hot grill. The result convinced her she was wrong and she was given a piece of persimmon to taste at leisure. This raised for the group questions about how people can be helped to change their minds – an issue central to education.

The foregoing exercises are not intended to be a substitute for a College of Education course on how people learn. They are simply examples of ways in which people who have not thought about the subject and who may have had a minimum of formal education can be helped to think about the subject and can help others also to think about it.

Appendix B

A CHURCH COMMUNITY COURSE
(By the Rev. J. P. Reardon, Secretary of the Church and Society
Department of the United Reformed Church.)

The term 'Use of Resources', might have been thrown up because of reports in a local paper of pollution or wastage of some resource(s) previously available for local use, or because of a Government report highlighting an issue, or because of a particular problem raised in conversation with the children, e.g., 'I've just had a fishing-rod for Christmas but there aren't any fish in the local river any more.'

Planning the Programme. In the planning stage, which should include those who will be responsible for project work with the children; adults who will lead groups; the minister or lay person who will lead worship, share in the leadership of project and discussion work, and act as a resource and co-ordinating person; leaders of church organizations; the organist or other musician(s). The group's first task will be to decide how best to handle the concern. In this case it might be decided to focus on the 'local river'.

In the initial planning stages, the course should be outlined in broad principles rather than in minute details, so that all sections of the church can contribute suggestions about how it can participate most fruitfully. It will be emphasized that the theme is a concern for the whole church. This fundamental dimension to the programme must be underlined in the way the course is worked out. Adults and children should be encouraged to share their insights with each other at every stage so that each group can learn from the others.

SUGGESTED PROGRAMME IN OUTLINE

Unit 1
A presentation of the local concern in as dramatic and visual a way as possible, with the whole church assembled together, e.g., an exhibition of material found in the river by a group from the church; slides of the river (showing clean upper reaches, and industrial waste being poured in, contrasted with the pictures of fishermen lower down the river trying to catch fish, etc.); an illustrated talk about the state of the river. An opportunity may then be given to the family to respond to what has been shown or said, e.g., buzz groups where people are sitting (impossible if churches insist on having children and adults separated); some quick reactions using a wandering microphone; a small panel of people who give their opinions about what has been said (they should not be told the detail of the presentation in advance, merely a warning that they will be called upon to give their views about pollution in their river). A short period follows in which

it is explained that during the week and next Sunday, the church will pursue different aspects of the main theme in groups, e.g., some will be asked to look at the river as a centre for leisure activities; some will look at damage that has been done to the river; others will look at the usefulness of the river in the life of the town; yet others will consider the way the river has played its part historically and what changes have taken place, perhaps even in their lifetime.

Family Worship follows emphasizing thanksgiving for God's gift of the world to mankind. The idea of man's stewardship as his response to God's goodness could also be included.

Unit 2

The session begins in separate groups to explore the specific themes allocated last week. Leaders in these groups will be looking for ways of distilling the essence of the work, or the discovery, or the discussion, for presentation to the whole church.

Sharing of findings: a twenty-minute presentation of the insights of the groups. (Children may have visited the river and taped an interview with a fisherman; adults may have talked about the beginning of their community as a convenient place to ford the river; if the river is large and important the youth group might have examined the way the river has figured in poetry and folk song, etc.)

The leader will draw the threads together noting how each group has been showing how important the river is in the community's life and how badly the river has been used and taken for granted.

Family Worship follows. Images of the river in the Bible might be used to show how God's love is made real to man – often in unexpected ways.

Unit 3

The session opens with Family Worship in which there is a celebration of God's gift of water. The Worship starts the church thinking of the river as a water resource (which man has spoilt). At the back of this there lies the conviction that Christians should be concerned about the river because:

(*a*) its pollution limits its use for others and spoils the pleasure it could othewise give;

(*b*) Christian stewardship speaks of the natural world as being God-given for us to enjoy, to pass on to others and as showing God's glory;

(*c*) it represents the livelihood of people in transport and in local industry;

(*d*) it is a water supply;

(*e*) if it is going to be systematically ru:ned it is a resource which can never be replaced – the ecological balance in the river must be maintained.

In groups (in various parts of the buildings) the 3–4 year olds play with water and play 'river' games. The 5–6 year old children explore what a fascinating thing a river is by means of pictures, games and activities. 7–10 year olds consider the problem of pollution through games and stories then meet someone who is trying to clean up the river, (e.g., a young person recently involved in a voluntary campaign). Adults and young people explore the effect of the present state of the river on people's livelihoods – how far is the pollution benefiting some at the expense of others? They will also look at the question of how far anything can be done to alter the present situation and what sort of pressures will make people respond positively.

Unit 4

Each group will look at what is being done in the present situation, e.g., adults, young people and 7–10s might be visited by local authority officials, local angling club spokesmen or local Civic Society representatives who will speak briefly about current projects. 5–6 and 3–4 year old children, through play, story and demonstration, learn about litter and also about how fish survive.

The Family Worship will include penitence, thanksgiving and commitment. The first week's visual display, etc., might be used again as a visual prayer. At the end of the service there should be made available ways in which people can demonstrate their concern further, e.g., petition forms; literature from interested societies; books to read; application forms for membership of National Trust, Civic Society, etc.

References

1. *Communication and the Christian Community.* H. A. Hamilton. Independent Press, 1961.
2. *Teaching the Christian Faith Today.* D. S. Hubery. Denholm House Press, 1965.
3. *The Story of the People of God.* Ed. R. S. Matthews. British Lessons Council, 1976.
4. *The Child in the Church.* British Council of Churches, 1976.
5. *A Rumour of Angels.* P. L. Berger. Pelican, 1971.
6. *Family Church Reappraised.* Congregation Church in England and Wales, 1965.
7. *On becoming a person.* C. Rogers. Constable, 1961.
8. *Six psychological studies.* J. Piaget. Vintage Books, New York.
My indebtedness to the work of Piaget is clearly evident in this chapter. It is my hope, however, that readers interested in the religious development of children would read also the work of Erik Erikson, Lawrence Kohlberg and John Fowler. Erikson's analysis of developmental stages is as follows:

Approximate age 0–1: Basic trust versus basic mistrust

2–3: Autonomy versus shame and doubt

4–5: Initiative versus guilt

6–12: Industry versus inferiority

12–18: Identity versus role confusion

Young Adulthood: Intimacy versus isolation

Adulthood: Generativity versus stagnation

Maturity: Integrity versus despair

Kohlberg's analysis of stages of moral development is as follows:
Stages 1 and 2 refer usually to the first nine to twelve years of life; stages 3 and 4 are accomplished by the age of twenty. It is said that three quarters of the adult population have not grown past stage four.

Level 1: Moral values reside in external happenings, acts and needs rather than in persons and standards.

Stage 1 – Punishment and obedience. A person accepts rules and defers to older people to avoid getting into trouble.

Stage 2 – Personal usefulness. A person accepts rules and obeys them in order to obtain rewards. Things are done for other people as a way of persuading them to do good things in return.

Level 2: Moral value resides in doing the right thing; conventions are upheld and the expectations of other people are fulfilled.

Stage 3 – Approval seeking. A person helps or tries to please in order to gain approval or to avoid disappointment. A sense of the proper thing to do is strong.

Stage 4 – Law and order. Respect for law and order and a sense of duty predominate. Value decisions are made in relation to the rules.

Level 3: Moral values are derived from principles which are held to be true. There is a sense of independence about the holding of principles.

Stage 5 – Social contract. Laws can be changed when they violate generally held principles. The will or welfare of the majority is important. Duty is thought of as a social contract.

Stage 6 – Conscience or principle. General ethical principles which apply everywhere are important. Moral choice is related to principles which are consistent and apply locally and universally.

John W. Fowler has been influenced by Piaget, Erikson and Kohlberg. As a result of many hundreds of interviews he has identified six steps in the development of faith (faith understood as a way of knowing and interpreting). These are:

Stage 1 – Ages 4 to 7 or 8. Intuitive faith. Communication largely through feelings.

Stage 2 – Ages 6 or 7 to 11 or 12. Literal faith. The authority of others is accepted. The child thinks concretely; the nurturing environment is important. Symbols or myths are related to the specific and the concrete.

Stage 3 – Ages 11 or 12 to 17. Conventional faith. The family, church, peers, school are supremely important. Symbols are no longer understood in relation to the specific and concrete. The expectations and judgments of others matter a great deal.

Stage 4 – Ages 17 to 20 onwards, but for some people not until the 30's or 40's. Reflective faith. Dependence on others for identity and faith decreases. A personal comprehensive world view is worked out and validated by the individual. Institutional religion may be seen as being too conventional or conformist.

Stage 5 – Age 30 plus. Consolidation of faith. A mid-life reflection involving a re-working of past attitudes and beliefs. A new appreciation of symbols, myths, rituals develops; paradoxes and tensions are accepted as part of understanding.

Stage 6 – Occurs only rarely. A universalizing of faith. An ability beyond that which is usual to integrate and universalize faith and experience.

9. *Age level characteristics compared.* Secretariat for Christian Education, Lutheran World Federation, 1975.

10. *Equipped to Teach.* United Reformed Church and Baptist Union of Great Britain & Ireland, 1973.

11. Note page 11, Dr. Hyde's qualification of Dr. Goldman's research and page 61, mention of Dr. Peatling's research.

12. *Teaching as a subversive activity.* Postman & Weingartner. Penguin Education, 1966.
13. *Hope and Planning.* J. Moltmann. SCM Press, 1971.
14. I am grateful to Ruben A. Alves for these insights. See his *Tomorrow's Child.* SCM Press, 1972.
15. *Christian Confidence.* Ed. R. Tomes. SPCK, 1970.
16. See *Religious Thinking from Childhood to Adolescence and Readiness for Religion.* R. Goldman. Routledge & Kegan Paul, 1964 and 1965.
17. John H. Peatling's work is summarized in 'On beyond Goldman: religious thinking and the 1970s' in *Learning for Living.* Spring 1977 (vol. 16 No. 3).
18. *The Teaching Methods of Jesus.* D. S. Hubery. CHP, 1970. See also the discussion of Jesus as teacher in *The Founder of Christianity* by C. H. Dodd. Collins, 1979.
19. *Little Owl Bible story book* 'The Man who Helped'. G. Stowell. Scripture Union, 1971.
20. *The parables of Jesus.* J. Jeremias. SCM Press, 1954.
21. *Christian Education and the Bible.* D. S. Hubery. REP, 1967.
22. *Readiness for Religion.* R. Goldman. Routledge & Kegan Paul, 1965.
23. *Teenage Religion.* H. Loukes. SCM Press, 1961.
24. *Christianity at the Centre.* J. Hick. SCM Press, 1968.
25. *Theology and Community Development.* A. J. Wesson. Privately circulated paper, 1973.
26. *Education for what is real.* G. D. Kelley. Harper & Row, 1947.
27. *Power for the powerless: The role of community action.* R. Holman. BCC, 1973.
28. *Building a better community.* Ed. A. Stevens. BCC (pamphlet), 1978.
29. *Cultural action for freedom.* P. Freire. Penguin Books, 1972.
30. *Brazil: A profile of poverty.* J. Edwards. Christian Aid, 1971.
31. In a paper on *Education and Theology,* published by the Christian Education Movement in 1973, the Rev. Prof. Peter Ackroyd says of theology: 'The day has passed when theology could simply expect to hold its place, and that a central one, by being regarded as the queen of the sciences. To claim for it an integrating function would also be to assume that it occupies a central position. But to see theology as a discipline of serious study which impinges on all areas of human experience, on all areas in which we are involved in the study of man, and the evaluation of his experience, and the assessment of his place, is not to make an arrogant claim. It is simply to ask educated men to take sufficient account of what through human history has been seen as an essential element, whether or not expressed in the formalised style of creed or church, an area in which questions are asked and replies are formulated which demand serious consideration.'
32. *George Hamilton Archibald: Crusader for youth.* E. T. Johnston. REP, 1945.
33. *Communique of the programme unit III sub-unit on education.* Spring, 1978.

34. Prepared in 1973 for a Consultation arranged by the Church Life Department of the United Reformed Church.
35. I have been shown recently the aim for its church education programmes agreed in 1977 by the Evangelical Churches in the German Democratic Republic. It seems to me to be a particularly fine statement which acknowledges the special difficulties and opportunities of young Christians in East Germany. It nicely balances the gift of the gospel, individual responsibility, and the community of the church: 'As they accompany the congregation, children and young people should experience the Gospel as a liberating and orientating offer. In this way they should be helped to understand the world, to master their own lives and to live as members of the congregation. They should then learn to live as Christians in a socialist society, accountable to the Lord.'
36. *Contact poems*. C. Taylor. Galliard, 1972.
37. *Living Issues: Conflict.* J. M. Sutcliffe and P. Lee Woolf. SCM, 1971.
38. *Aids to teaching and learning.* H. Coppen. Pergamon Press, 1969.